SIFTED MACARON CO.

The ultimate guide to delightfully delicious macarons.

Randi Fahle

TABLE OF
CONTENTS

Vanilla

Lemon

Raspberry
Cheesecake

Introduction

Macarons are made of precise amounts of almond flour, sugar and egg whites. Found within these pages are my method, as plainly as I know how to explain it, and with as many tips as I have. Macarons should be light and slightly chewy and made from two cookies sandwiching a filling. Not to be confused with the Maracoon, which is just a clump of meringue and desiccated coconut.

A distinct feature of a macaron is the 'foot' or small ruffling of the batter at the base causing the shell to rise. The traditional macaron is round and about 1-1 ½ inch in diameter. Sifted Macarons are typically pushing 2 inches, because who doesn't love a few extra bites?

To be quite honest, I am just as surprised as you are to be holding this book, written by me, about macarons. I am a self-taught baker, who not only had no real desire to start a business, I hadn't even made a macaron until a month before I jumped delightfully into business.

If you are just here for the pictures – I get you. If you want to master macarons, I'm here for it. Macarons require baking intuition, some common sense and a lot of patience and perseverance. The range of colors and flavors of macarons are limited only by your imagination; however, I have made it my absolute mission to make macarons that not only look beautiful but taste delicious. You are not limited to the flavors in my book obviously, but I hope the recipes and pictures are a springboard to your creativity.

As many stories I think we will continue to hear for years to come, spring 2020 was defining. I got sent home to work through quarantine like millions of others, I was grateful to continue to have my job, but devastated to be stuck at home. What most people didn't know that leaving my home to go to work was a critical escape, an hour long commutes each way that allowed me to plan, and prepare. I used this time to give myself pep talks, or tried simply to put it on the shelf. I won't elaborate much further, but older child adoption from foster care x2 is really hard work, and attachment disorders are difficult to navigate and scary to experience.

A pivotal moment came Mother's Day that year. I was gifted a macaron cookbook; the rest is history. To be transparent, I'm not a big fan of recipes that require you to buy a lot of stuff. If I hadn't already owned a food scale it may have stopped me right there.

I first began making macarons and then would drop them on friends' porches, (remember it was quarentine). The lucky ladies would then weigh-in on the flavors via voice chat. One night after it was deemed safe to do so, we sat in a backyard, eating macarons and giving updates on life with our adoptive families. My very wise friend Laurie, said I should start a business. I said "no" and proceeded to give all the actual real-life reasons why that wasn't a good idea, "I don't know what I'm doing; this is a fluke", "I have a full-time job." But it was that suggestion that led to Sifted Macaron Co.

The name 'Sifted' is a term that comes from a baking process, it means to sort out what is useful or valuable. I think, it's an essential process, not just in macarons, or baking in general, but as a person. To pursue better, you must do the work. You must Sift. So as I work through deep grief and trauma, I'm sorting out what is useful. You are holding this book because Macarons are a really good example of what can come of doing. the. work.

I hope this book and my story inspires you. That you don't limit yourself based on what you have or haven't been taught or think you are caplable of. You are one new-thing away from finding what you were meant to do.

I hope this book sparks a desire to do something new, and to find a way to help others along the way.

Supplies, Ingredients & Secrets

THE SUPPLIES

Items you'll need to gather beforehand are as follows. Brand in my opinion doesn't particularly matter so I have not elaborated as they are more preference than anything. I own two kitchenaid mixers, one of which was a wedding gift from the catering company I worked for as a teen, the other was a gift. Just use what you have.

- (3) Half sheet baking pans
- Silicone Baking Mat, you'll need 2 1/2 mats when making my recipes
- Half sheet pre-cut parchment paper
- Handheld sift, fine mesh with handle
- Food processer, 10-14cup capacity
- Stand mixer, 4.5-5Quart capacity
- Wisk and Paddle attachment for stand mixer
- Spatula, flexible and nonstick
- 12 inch piping bags
- #10 metal piping tip
- Cupplers for cake decorating
- Electronic food scale
- Food color powder or gel
- Thin Cake tester
- Teaspoon and Tablespoon measuring spoons

THE INGREDIENTS & SECRETS

THE ALMOND

Almonds are an oily seed, and as I've come across the occasional macaron flop – the almond flour has been the source. We won't be making our own almond flour here, but you certainly can. I have made my own nut-free flour by roasting pumpkin seeds and milling them and oven drying the flour. But I won't go over that here. Buy your Almond flour and before you even begin trying to whip up macarons, you'll need to bake on a rimmed half cookie sheet lined with parchment paper at 200 degrees for 2-3 hours or more. Your flour might not look overly 'wet' out of the package, but I almost quit a year into my business because of 'wet' almond flour and I'm telling you - bake it first.

THE EGG

Egg whites are separated, weighed and 'dried'. I did attempt early on to use solely store-bought egg whites, and what I can tell you is that you can supplement pasteurized egg whites to meet the weight needed for the recipe, but you will not achieve stiff peaks using entirely boxed egg whites from the store. You can however use 4 egg whites and then use the boxed egg whites to reach your 165 grams needed. The egg whites are easier to separate if the eggs are room temperature first or warmed in a warm water bath. Once weighed, set aside loosely covered overnight. It can also be 4- 6hrs if you want to separate in the morning and bake in the evening. This is how you dry out your egg whites.

GRANULATED SUGAR & POWDERED SUGAR

Not much elaboration needed here. I've used all brands of both with no issue. I will say that when dialing in my recipe – the consistency came down to the balance of both. Powdered sugar increased in a recipe certainly lends to the smoothness, but also can tip to a runny batter rather quickly and granulated sugar levels lead to stable meringue and is also essential.

FOOD COLOR POWDER OR GEL

SugarArt brand powder lends to more vibrant colors without adding liquid to your already delicate meringue, while gel is more readily available at your supermarket, the color is more subtle, as you don't want to add much more than a few drops.

A few notes;

Oil will be your worse nightmare, make sure all your mixing bowles and utencils are clean. You may also need to wipe down your silicon mats with vinegar if used previously.

Secondly; remember Macarons don't care about your feelings. Neither do sprinkles.

SIFTED CLASSICS

Cake Macaron

A classic white cake batter flavor and all the color and sprinkle flare to elicit iced animal cracker excitement. An original Sifted Macaron, its been hanging around since the beginning of time.

Makes | 30 macarons

FOR THE SHELLS

- 165g egg whites
- 136g caster sugar
- 180g almond flour
- 174.5g powdered sugar
- 1/16 tsp hot pink food color powder
- Rainbow nonpareil sprinkles

FOR THE FILLING

- 2 sticks salted butter, room temperature
- 2.5 cups powdered sugar
- 1.5 tsp. cake batter flavoring
- ¼ cup rainbow jimmies sprinkles

DIRECTIONS

1. Line a baking sheet with a silicon mat. Fit a piping bag with a cuppler and then a piping tip.

2. Grab a mixing bowl with measured and dried egg whites done earlier in the day. Whisk in the mixer until stiff peaks form, adding food color powder during this process.

3. In your food processor bowl, combine your dried and cooled almond flour along with your powdered sugar. Pulse a few times to combine, stir and pulse a few more times to fully combine.

4. Remove your bowl of stiff meringue, place sifter over bowl and add half dry ingredient mixture and sifting on top of meringue. Fold in lightly with a spatula, scraping around the bowl then through the center. Sift remaining dry ingredients and incorporate this same way, using the spatula to scrape around the bowl and then through the center. When this stirring or macaronage is complete, batter will fall in a smooth ribbon when lifted with the spatula.

5. Place piping bag with tip into a large mug or cup to hold as you pour half of batter pipe rounds into the center of the baking mat circle outlines. Hold piping bag perpendicular to the mat, squeeze steadily. To stop flow, stop squeezing and swipe quickly to create a smooth top. Once entire pan is piped, tap pan using both hands 2-3 times against table, then use cake tester to pop air bubbles and swirl to make top smooth. Sprinkle with nonpareils.

6. Preheat oven to 300, an internal oven thermometer will help as you will want to find out if your oven runs hot or cold. You may need to set your oven at 305, to get the internal thermometer to 300. This will take some adjustments.

7. Set pan aside to dry. You will want to touch the top of the cookie to ensure slightly firm and dry before baking.

8. Bake at 300 degrees for 18 minutes on middle rack, each sheet pan must be baked separately.

9. While macarons cool, beat butter in stand mixer using the paddle attachment. You will want the butter to be room temperature and it will be pale and fluffy when done. It is best to let it whip and go do something else. Add remaining buttercream ingredients when proper whipped butter has been achieved. Put into a piping bag and match macaron cookies and fill.

Fruity Cereal Macaron

A spoonful experience, sprinkled on top and filled with fruity cereal (cause I don't want to be sued) and milk buttercream.

Makes | 30 macarons

FOR THE SHELLS

- 165g egg whites
- 136g caster sugar
- 180g almond flour
- 174.5g powdered sugar
- 1/32 tsp lime green food powder
- Sprinkled with slightly crushed up fruity cereal

FOR THE FILLING

- 2 sticks salted butter, room temperature
- 3 cups powdered sugar
- 2 Tbs heavy whipping cream
- 1 cup crushed fruity cereal

DIRECTIONS

1. Line a baking sheet with a silicon mat. Fit a piping bag with a cuppler and then a piping tip.

2. Grab a mixing bowl with measured and dried egg whites done earlier in the day. Whisk in the mixer until stiff peaks form, adding food color powder during this process.

3. In your food processor bowl, combine your dried and cooled almond flour along with your powdered sugar. Pulse a few times to combine, stir and pulse a few more times to fully combine.

4. Remove your bowl of stiff meringue, place sifter over bowl and add half dry ingredient mixture and sifting on top of meringue. Fold in lightly with a spatula, scraping around the bowl then through the center. Sift remaining dry ingredients and incorporate this same way, using the spatula to scrape around the bowl and then through the center. When this stirring or macaronage is complete, batter will fall in a smooth ribbon when lifted with the spatula.

5. Place piping bag with tip into a large mug or cup to hold as you pour half of batter pipe rounds into the center of the baking mat circle outlines. Hold piping bag perpendicular to the mat, squeeze steadily.

6. To stop flow, stop squeezing and swipe quickly to create a smooth top. Once entire pan is piped, tap pan using both hands 2-3 times against table, then use cake tester to pop air bubbles and swirl to make top smooth. Sprinkle with nonpareils.

7. Preheat oven to 300, an internal oven thermometer will help as you will want to find out if your oven runs hot or cold. You may need to set your over at 305, to get the internal thermometer to 300. This will take some adjustments.

8. Set pan aside to dry. You will want to touch the top of the cookie to ensure slightly firm and dry before baking.

9. Bake at 300 degrees for 18 minutes on middle rack, each sheet pan must be baked separately.

10. While macarons cool, beat butter in stand mixer using the paddle attachment. You will want the butter to be room temperature and it will be pale and fluffy when done. It is best to let it whip and go do something else. Add remaining buttercream ingredients when proper whipped butter has been achieved. Put into a piping bag and match macaron cookies and fill.

Cotton Candy Macaron

Its real childish and real good. The dual colored butter cream and cotton candy sprinkles help invoke the county fair feel.

Makes | 30 macarons

FOR THE SHELLS

- 165g egg whites
- 136g caster sugar
- 180g almond flour
- 174.5g powdered sugar
- 1/64 tsp each of French blue, Hawaiian blue, and sapphire sky food color powder
- Sprinkled with cotton candy flavored sprinkles

FOR THE FILLING

- 2 sticks salted butter, room temperature
- 3 cups powdered sugar
- 1 tsp cotton candy flavoring
  After making buttercream, split batch into two bowls and color using pink/blue or blue/purple. Place each color in its own bag, and then insert both into a larger bag to pipe together.

DIRECTIONS

1. Line a baking sheet with a silicon mat. Fit a piping bag with a cuppler and then a piping tip.

2. Grab a mixing bowl with measured and dried egg whites done earlier in the day. Whisk in the mixer until stiff peaks form, adding food color powder during this process.

3. In your food processor bowl, combine your dried and cooled almond flour along with your powdered sugar. Pulse a few times to combine, stir and pulse a few more times to fully combine.

4. Remove your bowl of stiff meringue, place sifter over bowl and add half dry ingredient mixture and sifting on top of meringue. Fold in lightly with a spatula, scraping around the bowl then through the center. Sift remaining dry ingredients and incorporate this same way, using the spatula to scrape around the bowl and then through the center. When this stirring or macaronage is complete, batter will fall in a smooth ribbon when lifted with the spatula.

5. Place piping bag with tip into a large mug or cup to hold as you pour half of batter pipe rounds into the center of the baking mat circle outlines. Hold piping bag perpendicular to the mat, squeeze steadily. To stop flow, stop squeezing and swipe quickly to create a smooth top. Once entire pan is piped, tap pan using both hands 2-3 times against table, then use cake tester to pop air bubbles and swirl to make top smooth. Sprinkle with cotton candy sprinkles

6. Preheat oven to 300, an internal oven thermometer will help as you will want to find out if your oven runs hot or cold. You may need to set your over at 305, to get the internal thermometer to 300. This will take some adjustments.

7. Set pan aside to dry. You will want to touch the top of the cookie to ensure slightly firm and dry before baking.

8. Bake at 300 degrees for 18 minutes on middle rack, each pan baked separately.

9. While macarons cool, beat butter in stand mixer using the paddle attachment. You will want the butter to be room temperature and it will be pale and fluffy when done. It is best to let it whip and go do something else. Add remaining buttercream ingredients when proper whipped butter has been achieved. Put into a piping bag and match macaron cookies and fill.

Fluffernutter Macaron

Part Peanut butter, Part Marshmallow. Learn how to pipe dual buttercream with this combo.

Makes | 30 macarons

FOR THE SHELLS

- 165g egg whites
- 136g caster sugar
- 180g almond flour
- 174.5g powdered sugar
- 1/32 tsp french blue food color powder

FOR THE PB FILLING

- 2 sticks salted butter, room temperature
- 2.5 cups powdered sugar 1 ¼ cup peanut butter

MARSHMALLOW FILLING

- 2 sticks salted butter, room temperature
- 2.5 cups powdered sugar 8 oz marshmallow fluff

DIRECTIONS

1. Line a baking sheet with a silicon mat. Fit a piping bag with a cuppler and then a piping tip.

2. Grab a mixing bowl with measured and dried egg whites done earlier in the day. Whisk in the mixer until stiff peaks form, adding food color powder during this process.

3. In your food processor bowl, combine your dried and cooled almond flour along with your powdered sugar. Pulse a few times to combine, stir and pulse a few more times to fully combine.

4. Remove your bowl of stiff meringue, place sifter over bowl and add half dry ingredient mixture and sifting on top of meringue. Fold in lightly with a spatula, scraping around the bowl then through the center. Sift remaining dry ingredients and incorporate this same way, using the spatula to scrape around the bowl and then through the center. When this stirring or macaronage is complete, batter will fall in a smooth ribbon when lifted with the spatula.

5. Place piping bag with tip into a large mug or cup to hold as you pour half of batter pipe rounds into the center of the baking mat circle outlines. Hold piping bag perpendicular to the mat, squeeze steadily.

To stop flow, stop squeezing and swipe quickly to create a smooth top. Once entire pan is piped, tap pan using both hands 2-3 times against table, then use cake tester to pop air bubbles.

6. Preheat oven to 300, an internal oven thermometer will help as you will want to find out if your oven runs hot or cold. You may need to set your over at 305, to get the internal thermometer to 300. This will take some adjustments.

7. Set pan aside to dry. You will want to touch the top of the cookie to ensure slightly firm and dry before baking.

8. Bake at 300 degrees for 18 minutes on middle rack, each pan baked separately.

9. While macarons cool, beat butter in stand mixer using the paddle attachment. You will want the butter to be room temperature and it will be pale and fluffy when done. It is best to let it whip and go do something else. Add remaining buttercream ingredients when proper whipped butter has been achieved. Put into a piping bag and match macaron cookies and fill by taking two lightly filled bags of each butter cream, placing together in a larger piping bag.

Cookie Dough Macaron

Cookie monster would be proud, a blue macaron filled with gluten free, egg free cookie dough filling.

Makes | 30 macarons

FOR THE SHELLS

- 165g egg whites
- 136g caster sugar
- 180g almond flour
- 174.5g powdered sugar
- 1/64 tsp Sapphire sky food color powder
- 1/64 tsp Blueberry food color powder

FOR THE FILLING

- 2 sticks salted butter, room temperature
- 1 cup brown sugar
- 1/5 cup caster sugar
- 1 cup almond flour
- 1/5 mini chocolate chips, chopped

DIRECTIONS

1. Line a baking sheet with a silicon mat. Fit a piping bag with a cuppler and then a piping tip.

2. Grab a mixing bowl with measured and dried egg whites done earlier in the day. Whisk in the mixer until stiff peaks form, adding food color powder during this process.

3. In your food processor bowl, combine your dried and cooled almond flour along with your powdered sugar. Pulse a few times to combine, stir and pulse a few more times to fully combine.

4. Remove your bowl of stiff meringue, place sifter over bowl and add half dry ingredient mixture and sifting on top of meringue. Fold in lightly with a spatula, scraping around the bowl then through the center. Sift remaining dry ingredients and incorporate this same way, using the spatula to scrape around the bowl and then through the center. When this stirring or macaronage is complete, batter will fall in a smooth ribbon when lifted with the spatula.

5. Place piping bag with tip into a large mug or cup to hold as you pour half of batter pipe rounds into the center of the baking mat circle outlines. Hold piping bag perpendicular to the mat, squeeze steadily. To stop flow, stop squeezing and swipe quickly to create a smooth top. Once entire pan is piped, tap pan using both hands 2-3 times against table, then use cake tester to pop air bubbles and swirl to make top smooth.

6. Preheat oven to 300, an internal oven thermometer will help as you will want to find out if your oven runs hot or cold. You may need to set your over at 305, to get the internal thermometer to 300. This will take some adjustments.

7. Set pan aside to dry. You will want to touch the top of the cookie to ensure slightly firm and dry before baking.

8. Bake at 300 degrees for 18 minutes on middle rack, each pan baked separately.

9. While macarons cool, beat butter in stand mixer using the paddle attachment. You will want the butter to be room temperature and it will be pale and fluffy when done. It is best to let it whip and go do something else. Add remaining cookie dough filling ingredients when proper whipped butter has been achieved. Put into a piping bag and match macaron cookies and fill.

Sugar Cookie Macaron

Classic iced sugar cookie vibes, decorated for any holiday, a hint of almond extract give this icing an elevated taste.

Makes | 30 macarons

FOR THE SHELLS

- 165g egg whites
- 136g caster sugar
- 180g almond flour
- 174.5g powdered sugar
- ¼ tsp white food color powder
- Sequin confetti sprinkles

FOR THE FILLING

- 2 sticks salted butter, room temperature
- 2.5 cups powdered sugar
- 1/8 tsp almond extract
- 1 tsp vanilla extract

DIRECTIONS

1. Line a baking sheet with a silicon mat. Fit a piping bag with a cuppler and then a piping tip.

2. Grab a mixing bowl with measured and dried egg whites done earlier in the day. Whisk in the mixer until stiff peaks form, adding food color powder during this process.

3. In your food processor bowl, combine your dried and cooled almond flour along with your powdered sugar. Pulse a few times to combine, stir and pulse a few more times to fully combine.

4. Remove your bowl of stiff meringue, place sifter over bowl and add half dry ingredient mixture and sifting on top of meringue. Fold in lightly with a spatula, scraping around the bowl then through the center. Sift remaining dry ingredients and incorporate this same way, using the spatula to scrape around the bowl and then through the center. When this stirring or macaronage is complete, batter will fall in a smooth ribbon when lifted with the spatula.

5. Place piping bag with tip into a large mug or cup to hold as you pour half of batter pipe rounds into the center of the baking mat circle outlines. Hold piping bag perpendicular to the mat, squeeze steadily. To stop flow, stop squeezing and swipe quickly to create a smooth top. Once entire pan is piped, tap pan using both hands 2-3 times against table, then use cake tester to pop air bubbles and swirl to make top smooth. Sprinkle with confetti sprinkles, can use color themed for any holiday for a festive touch.

6. Preheat oven to 300, an internal oven thermometer will help as you will want to find out if your oven runs hot or cold. You may need to set your over at 305, to get the internal thermometer to 300. This will take some adjustments.

7. Set pan aside to dry. You will want to touch the top of the cookie to ensure slightly firm and dry before baking.

8. Bake at 300 degrees for 18 minutes on middle rack, each pan baked separately.

9. While macarons cool, beat butter in stand mixer using the paddle attachment. You will want the butter to be room temperature and it will be pale and fluffy when done. It is best to let it whip and go do something else. Add remaining buttercream ingredients when proper whipped butter has been achieved. Put into a piping bag and match macaron cookies and fill.

Marshmallow Macaron

A magically delicious macaron, filled with dehydrated marshmallow buttercream.

Makes | 30 macarons

FOR THE SHELLS

- 165g egg whites
- 136g caster sugar
- 180g almond flour
- 174.5g powdered sugar
- ¼ tsp. white food color powder
- Crushed dehydrated marshmallows for sprinkles

FOR THE FILLING

- 2 sticks salted butter, room temperature
- 2 cups powdered sugar
- 8 oz. marshmallow fluff
- 1 ¼ cup dehydrated marshmallows whole

DIRECTIONS

1. Line a baking sheet with a silicon mat. Fit a piping bag with a cuppler and then a piping tip.

2. Grab a mixing bowl with measured and dried egg whites done earlier in the day. Whisk in the mixer until stiff peaks form, adding food color powder.

3. In your food processor bowl, combine your dried and cooled almond flour along with your powdered sugar. Pulse a few times to combine, stir and pulse a few more times to fully combine.

4. Remove your bowl of stiff meringue, place sifter over bowl and add half dry ingredient mixture and sifting on top of meringue. Fold in lightly with a spatula, scraping around the bowl then through the center. Sift remaining dry ingredients and incorporate this same way, using the spatula to scrape around the bowl and then through the center. When this stirring or macaronage is complete, batter will fall in a smooth ribbon when lifted with the spatula.

5. Place piping bag with tip into a large mug or cup to hold as you pour half of batter pipe rounds into the center of the baking mat circle outlines. Hold piping bag perpendicular to the mat, squeeze steadily. To stop flow, stop squeezing and swipe quickly to create a smooth top. Once entire pan is piped, tap pan using both hands 2-3 times against table, then use cake tester to pop air bubbles and swirl to make top smooth. Sprinkle with crushed marshmallows.

6. Preheat oven to 300, an internal oven thermometer will help as you will want to find out if your oven runs hot or cold. You may need to set your over at 305, to get the internal thermometer to 300. This will take some adjustments.

7. Set pan aside to dry. You will want to touch the top of the cookie to ensure slightly firm and dry before baking.

8. Bake at 300 degrees for 18 minutes on middle rack, each pan baked separately.

9. While macarons cool, beat butter in stand mixer using the paddle attachment. You will want the butter to be room temperature and it will be pale and fluffy when done. It is best to let it whip and go do something else. Add remaining buttercream ingredients when proper whipped butter has been achieved. Put into a piping bag and match macaron cookies and fill.

Watermelon Macaron

A dual color shell design is what makes this macaron stand out. The Watermelon punch buttercream is tart and a fun desert for summer.

Makes | 30 macarons

FOR THE RED SHELLS

- 165g egg whites
- 136g caster sugar
- 180g almond flour
- 174.5g powdered sugar
- 2 1/8 tsp Red Rose food color powder
- Black sesame seeds for sprinkles

FOR THE GREEN SHELLS

- 165g egg whites
- 136g caster sugar
- 180g almond flour
- 174.5g powdered sugar
- 1/8 tsp emerald green food color powder

FOR THE FILLING

- 2 sticks salted butter, room temperature
- 2.5 cups powdered sugar
- 2.15g Kool-Aid watermelon drink mix

DIRECTIONS

1. Line a baking sheet with a silicon mat. Fit a piping bag with a cuppler and then a piping tip.

2. Grab a mixing bowl with measured and dried egg whites done earlier in the day. Whisk in the mixer until stiff peaks form, adding food color powder during this process.

3. In your food processor bowl, combine your dried and cooled almond flour along with your powdered sugar. Pulse a few times to combine, stir and pulse a few more times to fully combine.

4. Remove your bowl of stiff meringue, place sifter over bowl and add half dry ingredient mixture and sifting on top of meringue. Fold in lightly with a spatula, scraping around the bowl then through the center. Sift remaining dry ingredients and incorporate this same way, using the spatula to scrape around the bowl and then through the center. When this stirring or macaronage is complete, batter will fall in a smooth ribbon when lifted with the spatula.

5. Place piping bag with tip into a large mug or cup to hold as you pour half of batter pipe rounds into the center of the baking mat circle outlines. Hold piping bag perpendicular to the mat, squeeze steadily. To stop flow, stop squeezing and swipe quickly to create a smooth top. Once entire pan is piped, tap pan using both hands 2-3 times against table, then use cake tester to pop air bubbles and swirl to make top smooth. Sprinkle red shells sparingly with black sesame seeds.

6. Preheat oven to 300, an internal oven thermometer will help as you will want to find out if your oven runs hot or cold. You may need to set your over at 305, to get the internal thermometer to 300. This will take some adjustments.

7. Set pan aside to dry. You will want to touch the top of the cookie to ensure slightly firm and dry before baking.

8. Bake at 300 degrees for 18 minutes on middle rack, each pan baked separately.

9. While macarons cool, beat butter in stand mixer using the paddle attachment. You will want the butter to be room temperature and it will be pale and fluffy when done. It is best to let it whip and go do something else. Add remaining buttercream ingredients when proper whipped butter has been achieved. Put into a piping bag and match macaron cookies and fill.

NUTS

Maple Pecan Macaron

Midwest Autum in your mouth. You can't go wrong with a homemade pecan praline center wrapped up with maple buttercream.

Makes | 30 macarons

FOR THE SHELLS

- 165g egg whites
- 136g caster sugar
- 180g almond flour
- 174.5g powdered sugar
- 1/16 tsp redwood food color powder

FOR THE BUTTERCREAM FILLING

- 2 sticks salted butter, room temperature
- 2.5 cups powdered sugar
- ¾ tsp maple extract
- 1 Tbs maple syrup

FOR THE PECAN PRALINE FILLING

- 2/3 cup brown sugar 1/3 cup caster sugar 1 tsp cinnamon
- 2 tsp salt
- 1 pound pecan pieces
- 1 egg white, room temperature and beaten till frothy
- *Add pecans to egg whites to coat, then add dry ingredients and toss to combine. Place on a parchment covered baking pan. Bake 325 for 20 minutes. Stir halfway through.

DIRECTIONS

1. Line a baking sheet with a silicon mat. Fit a piping bag with a cuppler and then a piping tip.

2. Grab a mixing bowl with measured and dried egg whites done earlier in the day. Whisk in the mixer until stiff peaks form, adding food color powder during this process.

3. In your food processor bowl, combine your dried and cooled almond flour along with your powdered sugar. Pulse a few times to combine, stir and pulse a few more times to fully combine.

4. Remove your bowl of stiff meringue, place sifter over bowl and add half dry ingredient mixture and sifting on top of meringue. Fold in lightly with a spatula, scraping around the bowl then through the center. Sift remaining dry ingredients and incorporate this same way, using the spatula to scrape around the bowl and then through the center. When this stirring or macaronage is complete, batter will fall in a smooth ribbon when lifted with the spatula.

5. Place piping bag with tip into a large mug or cup to hold as you pour half of batter pipe rounds into the center of the baking mat circle outlines. Hold piping bag perpendicular to the mat, squeeze steadily.

To stop flow, stop squeezing and swipe quickly to create a smooth top. Once entire pan is piped, tap pan using both hands 2-3 times against table, then use cake tester to pop air bubbles and swirl to make top smooth.

6. Preheat oven to 300, an internal oven thermometer will help as you will want to find out if your oven runs hot or cold. You may need to set your over at 305, to get the internal thermometer to 300. This will take some adjustments.

7. Set pan aside to dry. You will want to touch the top of the cookie to ensure slightly firm and dry before baking.

8. Bake at 300 degrees for 18 minutes on middle rack, each pan baked separately.

9. While macarons cool, beat butter in stand mixer using the paddle attachment. You will want the butter to be room temperature and it will be pale and fluffy when done. It is best to let it whip and go do something else. Add remaining buttercream ingredients when proper whipped butter has been achieved. Put into a piping bag. No buttercream barrier needed for this recipe. Circle that buttercream and fill with a few small pecan pieces.

PB Pretzel Macaron

All the chewy, crunchy and creamy textures are here. Love your chocolate and salty prezels too? This ones for you.

Makes | 30 macarons

FOR THE SHELLS

- 165g egg whites
- 136g caster sugar
- 180g almond flour
- 174.5g powdered sugar
- 1/8 tsp blue spruce food color powder

FOR THE FILLING

- 2 sticks salted butter, room temperature
- 2.5 cups powdered sugar 1 ¼ cup peanut butter
- Gluten free chocolate covered pretzels to sandwich in

DIRECTIONS

1. Line a baking sheet with a silicon mat. Fit a piping bag with a cuppler and then a piping tip.

2. Grab a mixing bowl with measured and dried egg whites done earlier in the day. Whisk in the mixer until stiff peaks form, adding food color powder during this process.

3. In your food processor bowl, combine your dried and cooled almond flour along with your powdered sugar. Pulse a few times to combine, stir and pulse a few more times to fully combine.

4. Remove your bowl of stiff meringue, place sifter over bowl and add half dry ingredient mixture and sifting on top of meringue. Fold in lightly with a spatula, scraping around the bowl then through the center. Sift remaining dry ingredients and incorporate this same way, using the spatula to scrape around the bowl and then through the center. When this stirring or macaronage is complete, batter will fall in a smooth ribbon when lifted with the spatula.

5. Place piping bag with tip into a large mug or cup to hold as you pour half of batter pipe rounds into the center of the baking mat circle outlines. Hold piping bag perpendicular to the mat, squeeze steadily. To stop flow, stop squeezing and swipe quickly to create a smooth top. Once entire pan is piped, tap pan using both hands 2-3 times against table, then use cake tester to pop air bubbles.

6. Preheat oven to 300, an internal oven thermometer will help as you will want to find out if your oven runs hot or cold. You may need to set your over at 305, to get the internal thermometer to 300. This will take some adjustments.

7. Set pan aside to dry. You will want to touch the top of the cookie to ensure slightly firm and dry before baking.

8. Bake at 300 degrees for 18 minutes on middle rack, each pan baked individually.

9. While macarons cool, beat butter in stand mixer using the paddle attachment. You will want the butter to be room temperature and it will be pale and fluffy when done. It is best to let it whip and go do something else. Add remaining buttercream ingredients when proper whipped butter has been achieved. Put into a piping bag and match macaron cookies and fill with a thin layer of buttercream, adding a chocolate covered pretzel, then a little dot of peanut butter buttercream on the opposite cookie to help stick.

PBJ Macaron

Is there a more nostalgic duo than this? I think not.

Makes | 30 macarons

FOR THE SHELLS

- 165g egg whites
- 136g caster sugar
- 180g almond flour
- 174.5g powdered sugar
- 1/32 tsp sapphire sky food color powder
- 2 1/16 tsp red rose food color powder

FOR THE FILLING

- 2 sticks salted butter, room temperature
- 2.5 cups powdered sugar
- 1 ¼ cup smooth peanut butter
- For the jelly filling Concord grape jelly

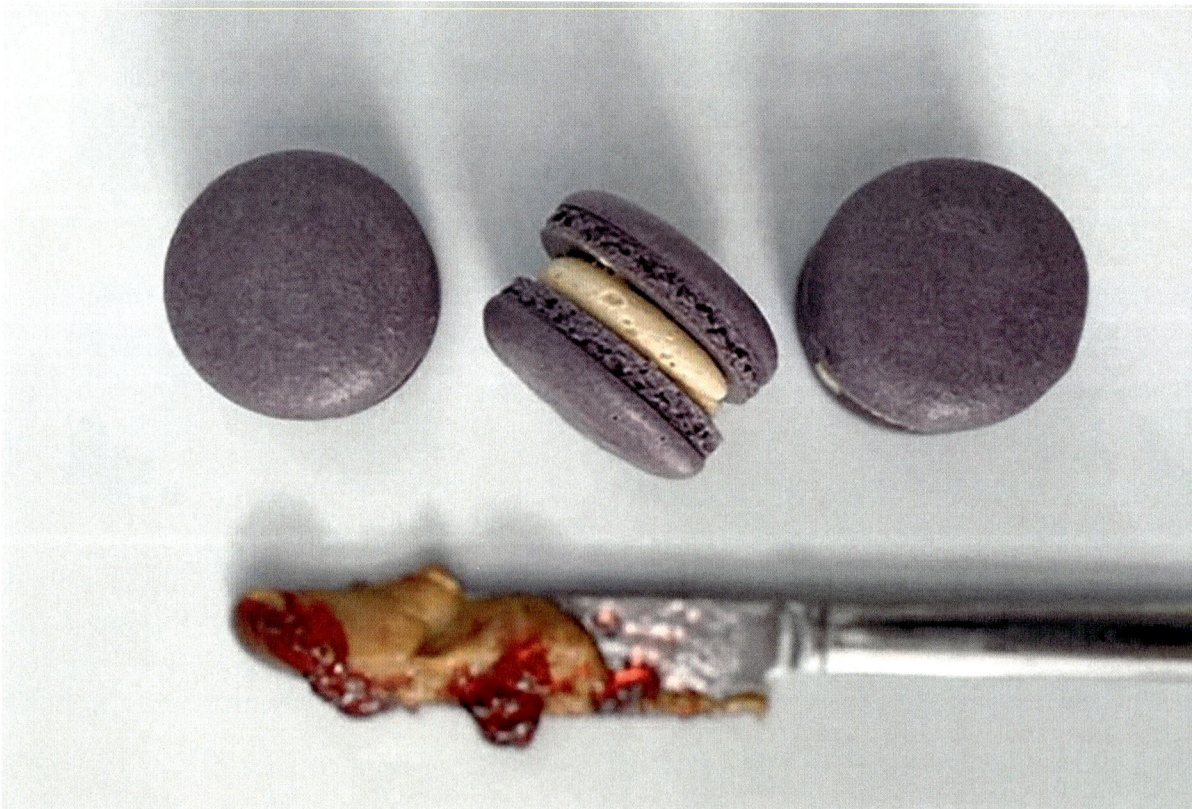

DIRECTIONS

1. Line a baking sheet with a silicon mat. Fit a piping bag with a cuppler and then a piping tip.

2. Grab a mixing bowl with measured and dried egg whites done earlier in the day. Whisk in the mixer until stiff peaks form, adding food color powder during this process.

3. In your food processor bowl, combine your dried and cooled almond flour along with your powdered sugar. Pulse a few times to combine, stir and pulse a few more times.

4. Remove your bowl of stiff meringue, place sifter over bowl and add half dry ingredient mixture and sifting on top of meringue. Fold in lightly with a spatula, scraping around the bowl then through the center. Sift remaining dry ingredients and incorporate this same way, using the spatula to scrape around the bowl and then through the center. When this stirring or macaronage is complete, batter will fall in a smooth ribbon when lifted with the spatula.

5. Place piping bag with tip into a large mug or cup to hold as you pour half of batter pipe rounds into the center of the baking mat circle outlines. Hold piping bag perpendicular to the mat, squeeze steadily. To stop flow, stop squeezing and swipe quickly to create a smooth top.

Once entire pan is piped, tap pan using both hands 2-3 times against table, then use cake tester to pop air bubbles.

6. Preheat oven to 300, an internal oven thermometer will help as you will want to find out if your oven runs hot or cold. You may need to set your over at 305, to get the internal thermometer to 300. This will take some adjustments.

7. Set pan aside to dry. You will want to touch the top of the cookie to ensure slightly firm and dry before baking.

8. Bake at 300 degrees for 18 minutes on middle rack, each pan baked individually.

9. While macarons cool, beat butter in stand mixer using the paddle attachment. You will want the butter to be room temperature and it will be pale and fluffy when done. It is best to let it whip and go do something else. Add remaining buttercream ingredients when proper whipped butter has been achieved. You will want to create a barrier by swiping a thin layer of buttercream on each shell before piping a circle of buttercream and filing with the grape jelly center. This will help cookie from leaking during maturation. Put into a piping bag and match macaron cookies and fill.

Pistachio Macaron

Sweet and Salty to perfection, this pistachio macaron is completely flavored by pistachios. No faking.

Makes | 30 macarons

FOR THE SHELLS

- 165g egg whites
- 136g caster sugar
- 180g almond flour
- 174.5g powdered sugar
- 1/8 tsp soldier green food color powder
- Chopped pistachios for sprinkles

FOR THE FILLING

- 2 sticks salted butter, room temperature
- 2.5 cups powdered sugar ¾ cup chopped pistachios ¾ tsp salt

DIRECTIONS

1. Line a baking sheet with a silicon mat. Fit a piping bag with a cuppler and then a piping tip.

2. Grab a mixing bowl with measured and dried egg whites done earlier in the day. Whisk in the mixer until stiff peaks form, adding food color powder during this process.

3. In your food processor bowl, combine your dried and cooled almond flour along with your powdered sugar. Pulse a few times to combine, stir and pulse a few more times to fully combine

4. Remove your bowl of stiff meringue, place sifter over bowl and add half dry ingredient mixture and sifting on top of meringue. Fold in lightly with a spatula, scraping around the bowl then through the center. Sift remaining dry ingredients and incorporate this same way, using the spatula to scrape around the bowl and then through the center. When this stirring or macaronage is complete, batter will fall in a smooth ribbon when lifted with the spatula.

5. Place piping bag with tip into a large mug or cup to hold as you pour half of batter pipe rounds into the center of the baking mat circle outlines. Hold piping bag perpendicular to the mat, squeeze steadily. To stop flow, stop squeezing and swipe quickly to create a smooth top. Once entire pan is piped, tap pan using both hands 2-3 times against table, then use cake tester to pop air bubbles. Sprinkle with chopped pistachios.

6. Preheat oven to 300, an internal oven thermometer will help as you will want to find out if your oven runs hot or cold. You may need to set your over at 305, to get the internal thermometer to 300. This will take some adjustments.

7. Set pan aside to dry. You will want to touch the top of the cookie to ensure slightly firm and dry before baking.

8. Bake at 300 degrees for 18 minutes on middle rack, each pan baked separately.

9. While macarons cool, beat butter in stand mixer using the paddle attachment. You will want the butter to be room temperature and it will be pale and fluffy when done. It is best to let it whip and go do something else. Add remaining buttercream ingredients when proper whipped butter has been achieved. Put into a piping bag and match and fill.

FRUIT

Apple Pie Macaron

An American classic, like an ala mode in macaron form.

Makes | 30 macarons

FOR THE SHELLS

- 165g egg whites
- 136g caster sugar
- 180g almond flour
- 174.5g powdered sugar
- 1/8 tsp soldier green food color powder
- ¼ tsp apple pie spice added to flour
- *Edible antique gold paint added after filling for design

FOR THE BUTTERCREAM FILLING

- 2 sticks salted butter, room temperature
- 3 cups powdered sugar 3 tsp vanilla bean paste

FOR THE APPLE FILLING

- 20oz can apple pie filling
- 1 Tbs caster sugar
- 1 Tbs brown sugar
- 1 Tbs apple pie spice

DIRECTIONS

1. Line a baking sheet with a silicon mat. Fit a piping bag with a cuppler and then a piping tip.

2. Grab a mixing bowl with measured and dried egg whites done earlier in the day. Whisk in the mixer until stiff peaks form, adding food color powder during this process.

3. In your food processor bowl, combine your dried and cooled almond flour along with your powdered sugar. Pulse a few times to combine, stir and pulse a few more times to fully combine.

4. Remove your bowl of stiff meringue, place sifter over bowl and add half dry ingredient mixture and sifting on top of meringue. Fold in lightly with a spatula, scraping around the bowl then through the center. Sift remaining dry ingredients and incorporate this same way, using the spatula to scrape around the bowl and then through the center. When this stirring or macaronage is complete, batter will fall in a smooth ribbon when lifted with the spatula.

5. Place piping bag with tip into a large mug or cup to hold as you pour half of batter pipe rounds into the center of the baking mat circle outlines. Hold piping bag perpendicular to the mat, squeeze steadily. To stop flow, stop squeezing and swipe quickly to create a smooth top. Once entire pan is piped, tap pan using both hands 2-3 times against table, then use cake tester to pop air bubbles and swirl to make top smooth.

6. Preheat oven to 300, an internal oven thermometer will help as you will want to find out if your oven runs hot or cold. You may need to set your over at 305, to get the internal thermometer to 300. This will take some adjustments.

7. Set pan aside to dry. You will want to touch the top of the cookie to ensure slightly firm and dry before baking.

8. Bake at 300 degrees for 18 minutes on middle rack, each pan baked separately.

9. While macarons cool, beat butter in stand mixer using the paddle attachment. You will want the butter to be room temperature and it will be pale and fluffy when done. It is best to let it whip and go do something else. Add remaining buttercream ingredients when proper whipped butter has been achieved. You will want to create a barrier by swiping a thin layer of buttercream on each shell before piping a circle of buttercream and filing with the apple center. This will help cookie from leaking during maturation. Match and filll.

Lemon Zest Macaron

A tart and sweet classic, the Lemon Zest Macaron has been on the Sifted menu since it began and uses lemon zest in the shell and butter cream. It's not the dish soap variety,

I promise.

Makes | 30 macarons

FOR THE SHELLS

- 165g egg whites
- 136g caster sugar
- 180g almond flour
- 174.5g powdered sugar
- 1 whole lemon zested (best if set out over night to dry if possible)
- 1/16 tsp sunshine yellow food color powder
- Yellow nonpareil sprinkles

FOR THE FILLING

- 2 sticks salted butter, room temperature
- 2.5 cups powdered sugar Zest of 2 lemons
- Juice of 2 lemons
- 1/64 tsp sunshine yellow food color powder

DIRECTIONS

1. Line a baking sheet with a silicon mat. Fit a piping bag with a cuppler and then a piping tip.

2. Grab a mixing bowl with measured and dried egg whites done earlier in the day. Whisk in the mixer until stiff peaks form, adding food color powder during this process.

3. In your food processor bowl, combine your dried and cooled almond flour along with your powdered sugar. Pulse a few times to combine, stir to fully combine and pulse a few more times to fully combine.

4. Remove your bowl of stiff meringue, place sifter over bowl and add half dry ingredient mixture and sifting on top of meringue. Fold in lightly with a spatula, scraping around the bowl then through the center. Sift remaining dry ingredients, for Lemon Zest specifically I sift some dry ingredients and sandwich in the zest. It helps with the lemon oil. Incorporate this same way, using the spatula to scrape around the bowl and then through the center. When this stirring or macaronage is complete, batter will fall in a smooth ribbon when lifted with the spatula.

5. Place piping bag with tip into a large mug or cup to hold as you pour half of batter pipe rounds into the center of the baking mat circle outlines. Hold piping bag perpendicular to the mat, squeeze steadily. To stop flow, stop squeezing and swipe quickly to create a smooth top. Once entire pan is piped, tap pan using both hands 2-3 times against table, then use cake tester to pop air bubbles. Sprinkle with yellow nonpareils.

6. Preheat oven to 300, an internal oven thermometer will help as you will want to find out if your oven runs hot or cold. You may need to set your over at 305, to get the internal thermometer to 300. This will take some adjustments.

7. Set pan aside to dry. You will want to touch the top of the cookie to ensure slightly firm and dry before baking.

8. Bake at 300 degrees for 18 minutes on middle rack, each pan baked separately.

9. While macarons cool, beat butter in stand mixer. You will want the butter to be room temperature and it will be pale and fluffy when done. It is best to let it whip and go do something else. Add remaining buttercream ingredients when proper whipped butter has been achieved. Put into a piping bag and match and fill.

Cheesecake Macaron

Cheesecake buttercream swirled around a tart raspberry center. Its divine.

Makes | 30 macarons

FOR THE SHELLS

165g egg whites

- 136g caster sugar
- 180g almond flour
- 174.5g powdered sugar
- 1/32 burgundy food color powder
- *Paint 1 stripe up the piping bag using red gel food color to produce an abstract look.

FOR THE CHEESECAKE FILLING

- 1 sticks salted butter, room temperature
- 1 block of cream cheese (whip creamcheese and butter together)
- 2.5 cups powdered sugar
- 1 pkg no-bake cheesecake mix with only ½ cup of milk (mixed separately and cooled before adding to whipped creamcheese/butter mixture.

FOR THE RASPBERRY CENTER

- 1 (11oz) jar of raspberry preserves
- 1 zested lime
- 1 Tbs caster sugar

DIRECTIONS

1. Line a baking sheet with a silicon mat. Fit a piping bag with a cuppler and then a piping tip.

2. Grab a mixing bowl with measured and dried egg whites done earlier in the day. Whisk in the mixer until stiff peaks form, adding food color powder during this process.

3. In your food processor bowl, combine your dried and cooled almond flour along with your powdered sugar. Pulse a few times to combine, stir and pulse a few more times to fully combine.

4. Remove your bowl of stiff meringue, place sifter over bowl and add half dry ingredient mixture and sifting on top of meringue. Fold in lightly with a spatula, scraping around the bowl then through the center. Sift remaining dry ingredients and incorporate this same way, using the spatula to scrape around the bowl and then through the center. When this stirring or macaronage is complete, batter will fall in a smooth ribbon when lifted with the spatula.

5. Place piping bag with tip into a large mug or cup to hold as you pour half of batter pipe rounds into the center of the baking mat circle outlines. Hold piping bag perpendicular to the mat, squeeze steadily.

The bag with one line of red color, will produce a cute abstract strip that looks like a lightning bolt. To stop flow, stop squeezing and swipe quickly to create a smooth top. Once entire pan is piped, tap pan using both hands 2-3 times against table, then use cake tester to pop air bubbles.

6. Preheat oven to 300, an internal oven thermometer will help as you will want to find out if your oven runs hot or cold. You may need to set your over at 305, to get the internal thermometer to 300. This will take some adjustments.

7. Set pan aside to dry. You will want to touch the top of the cookie to ensure slightly firm and dry before baking.

8. Bake at 300 degrees for 18 minutes on middle rack, each pan baked separately.

9. While macarons cool, make cheesecake buttercream and raspberry center. You will want to create a barrier by swiping a thin layer of buttercream on each shell before piping a circle of cream cheese buttercream and filing with the raspberry center. This will help cookie from leaking during maturation. Put into a piping bag and match cookies and fill.

Strawberry Macaron

A ripe off the vine taste, this macaron is filled with bright and fresh strawberry buttercream.

Makes | 30 macarons

FOR THE SHELLS

- 165g egg whites
- 136g caster sugar
- 180g almond flour
- 174.5g powdered sugar
- 1/8 tsp red rose food color powder
- Sprinkle with powdered freeze dried strawberries

FOR THE FILLING

- 2 sticks salted butter, room temperature
- 3 cups powdered sugar
- 28g powdered freeze dried strawberries
- 1 tsp. lime juice

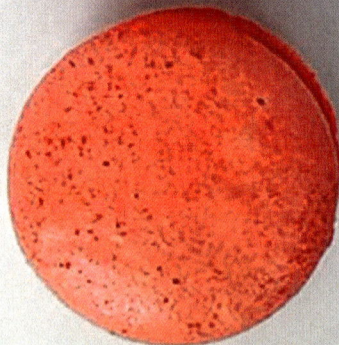

DIRECTIONS

1. Line a baking sheet with a silicon mat. Fit a piping bag with a cuppler and then a piping tip.

2. Grab a mixing bowl with measured and dried egg whites done earlier in the day. Whisk in the mixer until stiff peaks form, adding food color powder during this process.

3. In your food processor bowl, combine your dried and cooled almond flour along with your powdered sugar. Pulse a few times to combine, stir to fully combine and pulse a few more times to fully combine.

4. Remove your bowl of stiff meringue, place sifter over bowl and add half dry ingredient mixture and sifting on top of meringue. Fold in lightly with a spatula, scraping around the bowl then through the center. Sift remaining dry ingredients and incorporate this same way, using the spatula to scrape around the bowl and then through the center. When this stirring or macaronage is complete, batter will fall in a smooth ribbon when lifted with the spatula.

5. Place piping bag with tip into a large mug or cup to hold as you pour half of batter pipe rounds into the center of the baking mat circle outlines. Hold piping bag perpendicular to the mat, squeeze steadily.

To stop flow, stop squeezing and swipe quickly to create a smooth top. Once entire pan is piped, tap pan using both hands 2-3 times against table, then use cake tester to pop air bubbles and swirl to make top smooth. Sprinkle with powdered strawberries.

6. Preheat oven to 300, an internal oven thermometer will help as you will want to find out if your oven runs hot or cold. You may need to set your over at 305, to get the internal thermometer to 300. This will take some adjustments.

7. Set pan aside to dry. You will want to touch the top of the cookie to ensure slightly firm and dry before baking.

8. Bake at 300 degrees for 18 minutes on middle rack, each pan baked separately.

9. While macarons cool, beat butter in stand mixer using the paddle attachment. You will want the butter to be room temperature and it will be pale and fluffy when done. It is best to let it whip and go do something else. Add remaining buttercream ingredients when proper whipped butter has been achieved. Put into a piping bag and match macaron cookies and fill.

Cherry Almond Macaron

Maraschino cherry buttercream in an almond flavored shell. Its like an almond melt sugar cookie, classic and delicious.

Makes | 30 macarons

FOR THE SHELLS

- 165g egg whites
- 136g caster sugar
- 180g almond flour
- 174.5g powdered sugar
- ¼ tsp White food color powder
- Red jimmies sprinkles

FOR THE FILLING

- 2 sticks salted butter, room temperature
- 3 cups powdered sugar 1 tsp almond extract
- 5 Tbs maraschino cherry juice
- ½ Jar maraschino cherries, patted dry

DIRECTIONS

1. Line a baking sheet with a silicon mat. Fit a piping bag with a cuppler and then a piping tip.

2. Grab a mixing bowl with measured and dried egg whites done earlier in the day. Whisk in the mixer until stiff peaks form, adding food color powder during this process.

3. In your food processor bowl, combine your dried and cooled almond flour along with your powdered sugar. Pulse a few times to combine, stir to fully combine and pulse a few more times to fully combine.

4. Remove your bowl of stiff meringue, place sifter over bowl and add half dry ingredient mixture and sifting on top of meringue. Fold in lightly with a spatula, scraping around the bowl then through the center. Sift remaining dry ingredients and incorporate this same way, using the spatula to scrape around the bowl and then through the center. When this stirring or macaronage is complete, batter will fall in a smooth ribbon when lifted with the spatula.

5. Place piping bag with tip into a large mug or cup to hold as you pour half of batter pipe rounds into the center of the baking mat circle outlines. Hold piping bag perpendicular to the mat, squeeze steadily. To stop flow, stop squeezing and swipe quickly to create a smooth top. Once entire pan is piped, tap pan using both hands 2-3 times against table, then use cake tester to pop air bubbles. Sprinkle with red jimmies sprinkles.

6. Preheat oven to 300, an internal oven thermometer will help as you will want to find out if your oven runs hot or cold. You may need to set your over at 305, to get the internal thermometer to 300. This will take some adjustments.

7. Set pan aside to dry. You will want to touch the top of the cookie to ensure slightly firm and dry before baking.

8. Bake at 300 degrees for 18 minutes on middle rack, each sheet pan must be baked separately.

9. While macarons cool, beat butter in stand mixer using the paddle attachment. You will want the butter to be room temperature and it will be pale and fluffy when done. It is best to let it whip and go do something else. Add remaining buttercream ingredients when proper whipped butter has been achieved. Put into a piping bag and match macaron cookies and fill.

Orange Cream Macaron

Orange push-pop, orange zest sugar cookie vibes using orange zest and orange juice concentrate.

Makes | 30 macarons

FOR THE SHELLS

- 165g egg whites
- 136g caster sugar
- 180g almond flour
- 174.5g powdered sugar
- ¼ tsp White food color powder
- *Paint 3 stripes up the piping bag using orange gel food color to produce the swirl.

FOR THE FILLING

- 2 sticks salted butter, room temperature
- 3 cups powdered sugar
- 4 Tbs orange juice concentrate
- 1 orange zested

1. Line a baking sheet with a silicon mat. Fit a piping bag with a cuppler and then a piping tip.

2. Grab a mixing bowl with measured and dried egg whites done earlier in the day. Whisk in the mixer until stiff peaks form, adding food color powder during this process.

3. In your food processor bowl, combine your dried and cooled almond flour along with your powdered sugar. Pulse a few times to combine, stir to fully combine and pulse a few more times to fully combine.

4. Remove your bowl of stiff meringue, place sifter over bowl and add half dry ingredient mixture and sifting on top of meringue. Fold in lightly with a spatula, scraping around the bowl then through the center. Sift remaining dry ingredients and incorporate this same way, using the spatula to scrape around the bowl and then through the center. When this stirring or macaronage is complete, batter will fall in a smooth ribbon when lifted with the spatula.

5. Place piping bag with tip into a large mug or cup to hold as you pour half of batter, the bag has been striped with 3 orange gel lines, pipe rounds into the center of the baking mat circle outlines. Hold piping bag perpendicular to the mat, squeeze steadily.

The 3 stripes will produce an orange swirl. To stop flow, stop squeezing and swipe quickly to create a smooth top. Once entire pan is piped, tap pan using both hands 2-3 times against table, then use cake tester to pop air bubbles and swirl to make top smooth.

6. Preheat oven to 300, an internal oven thermometer will help as you will want to find out if your oven runs hot or cold. You may need to set your over at 305, to get the internal thermometer to 300. This will take some adjustments.

7. Set pan aside to dry. You will want to touch the top of the cookie to ensure slightly firm and dry before baking.

8. Bake at 300 degrees for 18 minutes on middle rack, each pan baked separately.

9. While macarons cool, beat butter in stand mixer using the paddle attachment. You will want the butter to be room temperature and it will be pale and fluffy when done. It is best to let it whip and go do something else. Add remaining buttercream ingredients when proper whipped butter has been achieved. Put into a piping bag and match macaron cookies and fill.

Lime Macaron

A subtle macaron, is fresh, its bright, its summer.

Makes | 30 macarons

FOR THE SHELLS

- 165g egg whites
- 136g caster sugar
- 180g almond flour
- 174.5g powdered sugar
- 1/16 tsp lime food color powder
- 2 limes zested (best if set out over night to dry if possible)

FOR THE FILLING

- 2 sticks salted butter, room temperature
- 2.5 cups powdered sugar
- 4 limes zested and juiced

DIRECTIONS

1. Line a baking sheet with a silicon mat. Fit a piping bag with a cuppler and then a piping tip.

2. Grab a mixing bowl with measured and dried egg whites done earlier in the day. Whisk in the mixer until stiff peaks form, adding food color powder during this process.

3. In your food processor bowl, combine your dried and cooled almond flour along with your powdered sugar. Pulse a few times to combine, stir to fully combine and pulse a few more times to fully combine.

4. Remove your bowl of stiff meringue, place sifter over bowl and add half dry ingredient mixture and sifting on top of meringue. Fold in lightly with a spatula, scraping around the bowl then through the center. Sift remaining dry ingredients and incorporate this same way, using the spatula to scrape around the bowl and then through the center. When this stirring or macaronage is complete, batter will fall in a smooth ribbon when lifted with the spatula.

5. Place piping bag with tip into a large mug or cup to hold as you pour half of batter pipe rounds into the center of the baking mat circle outlines. Hold piping bag perpendicular to the mat, squeeze steadily. To stop flow, stop squeezing and swipe quickly to create a smooth top. Once entire pan is piped, tap pan using both hands 2-3 times against table, then use cake tester to pop air bubbles and swirl to make top smooth.

6. Preheat oven to 300, an internal oven thermometer will help as you will want to find out if your oven runs hot or cold. You may need to set your over at 305, to get the internal thermometer to 300. This will take some adjustments.

7. Set pan aside to dry. You will want to touch the top of the cookie to ensure slightly firm and dry before baking.

8. Bake at 300 degrees for 18 minutes on middle rack, each sheet pan must be baked separately.

9. While macarons cool, beat butter in stand mixer using the paddle attachment. You will want the butter to be room temperature and it will be pale and fluffy when done. It is best to let it whip and go do something else. Add remaining buttercream ingredients when proper whipped butter has been achieved. Put into a piping bag and match macaron cookies and fill.

CHOCOLATES, CARMELS & COFFEE

Espresso Macaron

A real cup. This Espresso sprinkled macaron has espresso powder in the shell, sprinkled on top and filled with an espresso and marshmallow butter cream.

Makes | 30 macarons

FOR THE SHELLS

- 165g egg whites
- 136g caster sugar
- 180g almond flour
- 174.5g powdered sugar
- 1/8 tsp true brown food color powder
- 2.5g Medaglia D'Oro espresso powder + some to sprinkle on top

FOR THE FILLING

- 2 sticks salted butter, room temperature
- 2 cups powdered sugar 8 oz marshmallow fluff
- 4 tsp Medaglia D'Oro espresso powder

DIRECTIONS

1. Line a baking sheet with a silicon mat. Fit a piping bag with a cuppler and then a piping tip.

2. Grab a mixing bowl with measured and dried egg whites done earlier in the day. Whisk in the mixer until stiff peaks form, adding food color powder during this process.

3. In your food processor bowl, combine your dried and cooled almond flour along with your powdered sugar. Pulse a few times to combine, stir to fully combine and pulse a few more times to fully combine.

4. Remove your bowl of stiff meringue, place sifter over bowl and add half dry ingredient mixture and sifting on top of meringue. Fold in lightly with a spatula, scraping around the bowl then through the center. Sift remaining dry ingredients and incorporate this same way, using the spatula to scrape around the bowl and then through the center. When this stirring or macaronage is complete, batter will fall in a smooth ribbon when lifted with the spatula.

5. Place piping bag with tip into a large mug or cup to hold as you pour half of batter pipe rounds into the center of the baking mat circle outlines. Hold piping bag perpendicular to the mat, squeeze steadily. To stop flow, stop squeezing and swipe quickly to create a smooth top. Once entire pan is piped, tap pan using both hands 2-3 times against table, then use cake tester to pop air bubbles and swirl to make top smooth. Sprinkle lightly with espresso powder.

6. Preheat oven to 300, an internal oven thermometer will help as you will want to find out if your oven runs hot or cold. You may need to set your over at 305, to get the internal thermometer to 300. This will take some adjustments.

7. Set pan aside to dry. You will want to touch the top of the cookie to ensure slightly firm and dry before baking.

8. Bake at 300 degrees for 18 minutes on middle rack, each pan baked separately.

9. While macarons cool, beat butter in stand mixer using the paddle attachment. You will want the butter to be room temperature and it will be pale and fluffy when done. It is best to let it whip and go do something else. Add remaining buttercream ingredients when proper whipped butter has been achieved. Put into a piping bag and match macaron cookies and fill.

Chocolate PB Macaron

A chocolate shell filled with luscious peanut butter buttercream topped with crunchy chocolate sprinkles.

Makes | 30 macarons

FOR THE SHELLS

- 165g egg whites
- 136g caster sugar
- 180g almond flour
- 174.5g powdered sugar
- 1/8 tsp true brown food color powder
- ½ Tbs Cocoa powder
- Chopped peanuts or chocolate jimmies for sprinkles

FOR THE FILLING

- 2 sticks salted butter, room temperature
- 2.5 cups powdered sugar
- 1 ¼ Cup smooth peanut butter

DIRECTIONS

1. Line a baking sheet with a silicon mat. Fit a piping bag with a cuppler and then a piping tip.

2. Grab a mixing bowl with measured and dried egg whites done earlier in the day. Whisk in the mixer until stiff peaks form, adding food color powder during this process.

3. In your food processor bowl, combine your dried and cooled almond flour along with your powdered sugar. Pulse a few times to combine, stir to fully combine and pulse a few more times to fully combine.

4. Remove your bowl of stiff meringue, place sifter over bowl and add half dry ingredient mixture and sifting on top of meringue. Fold in lightly with a spatula, scraping around the bowl then through the center. Sift remaining dry ingredients and incorporate this same way, using the spatula to scrape around the bowl and then through the center. When this stirring or macaronage is complete, batter will fall in a smooth ribbon when lifted with the spatula.

5. Place piping bag with tip into a large mug or cup to hold as you pour half of batter pipe rounds into the center of the baking mat circle outlines. Hold piping bag perpendicular to the mat, squeeze steadily. To stop flow, stop squeezing and swipe quickly to create a smooth top. Once entire pan is piped, tap pan using both hands 2-3 times against table, then use cake tester to pop air bubbles and swirl to make top smooth. Sprinkle with chocolate jimmies sprinkles or chopped peanuts.

6. Preheat oven to 300, an internal oven thermometer will help as you will want to find out if your oven runs hot or cold. You may need to set your over at 305, to get the internal thermometer to 300. This will take some adjustments.

7. Set pan aside to dry. You will want to touch the top of the cookie to ensure slightly firm and dry before baking.

8. Bake at 300 degrees for 18 minutes on middle rack, each pan baked separately.

9. While macarons cool, beat butter in stand mixer using the paddle attachment. You will want the butter to be room temperature and it will be pale and fluffy when done. It is best to let it whip and go do something else. Add remaining buttercream ingredients when proper whipped butter has been achieved. Put into a piping bag and match macaron cookies and fill.

Salted Caramel Macaron

A Pink Himalayan salted macaron shell filled with homemade salted caramel, whipped to a piping perfection.

Makes | 30 macarons

FOR THE SHELLS

- 165g egg whites
- 136g caster sugar
- 180g almond flour
- 174.5g powdered sugar
- 1/32 tsp turquoise water food color powder
- 1/64 tsp blueberry food color powder
- Pink Himalayan flaked salt for sprinkles

FOR THE FILLING

- 200g heavy whipping cream
- 200g caster sugar
- 220g water
- Stick of softened butter
- 1 tsp salt

DIRECTIONS

1. Line a baking sheet with a silicon mat. Fit a piping bag with a cuppler and then a piping tip.

2. Grab a mixing bowl with measured and dried egg whites done earlier in the day. Whisk in the mixer until stiff peaks form, adding food color powder during this process.

3. In your food processor bowl, combine your dried and cooled almond flour along with your powdered sugar. Pulse a few times to combine, stir to fully combine and pulse a few more times to fully combine.

4. Remove your bowl of stiff meringue, place sifter over bowl and add half dry ingredient mixture and sifting on top of meringue. Fold in lightly with a spatula, scraping around the bowl then through the center. Sift remaining dry ingredients and incorporate this same way, using the spatula to scrape around the bowl and then through the center. When this stirring or macaronage is complete, batter will fall in a smooth ribbon when lifted with the spatula.

5. Place piping bag with tip into a large mug or cup to hold as you pour half of batter pipe rounds into the center of the baking mat circle outlines. Hold piping bag perpendicular to the mat, squeeze steadily. To stop flow, stop squeezing and swipe quickly to create a smooth top. Once entire pan is piped, tap pan using both hands 2-3 times against table, then use cake tester to pop air bubbles and swirl to make top smooth. Sprinkle with nonpareils.

6. Preheat oven to 300, an internal oven thermometer will help as you will want to find out if your oven runs hot or cold. You may need to set your over at 305, to get the internal thermometer to 300. This will take some adjustments.

7. Set pan aside to dry. You will want to touch the top of the cookie to ensure slightly firm and dry before baking.

8. Bake at 300 degrees for 18 minutes on middle rack, each sheet pan must be baked separately.

9. While macarons cool, make caramel by putting water and sugar into a saucepan. Bring to a simmer/boil until caramel brown is achieved. Add warmed heavy cream, then stirring in sliced butter periodically until fully incorporated. Cook over low heat for 18-20 minutes. Once fully cooled, whip in a stand mixer until fluffy and able to pipe.

Brownie Macaron

This chocolate shell filled with fudgy chocolate butter cream IS nostalgia, and one of my favorites.

Makes | 30 macarons

FOR THE SHELLS

- 165g egg whites
- 136g caster sugar
- 180g almond flour
- 174.5g powdered sugar
- ½ Tbs Cocoa Powder Cosmic brownie sprinkles
- (2) 1/8 True Brown Food color powder

FOR THE FILLING

- 2 sticks salted butter, room temperature
- 2.5 cups powdered sugar
- ½ cup cocoa powder
- 2 tsp vanilla extract
- 2 Tbs heavy whipping cream

DIRECTIONS

1. Line a baking sheet with a silicon mat. Fit a piping bag with a cuppler and then a piping tip.

2. Grab a mixing bowl with measured and dried egg whites done earlier in the day. Whisk in the mixer until stiff peaks form, adding food color powder during this process.

3. In your food processer bowl, combine your dried and cooled almond flour along with your powdered sugar. Pulse a few times to combine, stir to fully combine and pulse a few more times to fully combine.

4. Remove your bowl of stiff meringue, place sifter over bowl and add half dry ingredient mixture and sifting on top of meringue. Fold in lightly with a spatula, scraping around the bowl then through the center. Sift remaining dry ingredients and incorporate this same way, using the spatula to scrape around the bowl and then through the center. When this stirring or macaronage is complete, batter will fall in a smooth ribbon when lifted with the spatula.

5. Place piping bag with tip into a large mug or cup to hold as you pour half of batter pipe rounds into the center of the baking mat circle outlines. Hold piping bag perpendicular to the mat, squeeze steadily. To stop flow, stop squeezing and swipe quickly to create a smooth top. Once entire pan is piped, tap pan using both hands 2-3 times against table, then use cake tester to pop air bubbles and swirl to make top smooth. Sprinkle with cosmic brownie sprinkles.

6. Preheat oven to 300, an internal oven thermometer will help as you will want to find out if your oven runs hot or cold. You may need to set your over at 305, to get the internal thermometer to 300. This will take some adjustments.

7. Set pan aside to dry. You will want to touch the top of the cookie to ensure slightly firm and dry before baking.

8. Bake at 300 degrees for 18 minutes on middle rack, each sheet pan must be baked separately.

9. While macarons cool, beat butter in stand mixer using the paddle attachment. You will want the butter to be room temperature and it will be pale and fluffy when done. It is best to let it whip and go do something else. Add remaining buttercream ingredients when proper whipped butter has been achieved. Put into a piping bag and match macaron cookies and fill.

Chocolate Strawberry Macaron

A classic white cake batter flavor and all the color and sprinkle flare to elicit iced animal cracker excitement. An original Sifted Macaron, its been hanging around since the beginning of time.

Makes | 30 macarons

FOR THE SHELLS

- 165g egg whites
- 136g caster sugar
- 180g almond flour
- 174.5g powdered sugar
- 1/16 sassy pink food color powder

FOR THE FILLING

- 2 sticks salted butter, room temperature
- 2.5 cups powdered sugar
- ½ cup cocoa powder
- 3 Tbs heavy whipping cream

STRAWBERRY CENTER FILLING

- 1 pkg freeze dried strawberries powdered
- 1 pkg gelatin – unflavored water

DIRECTIONS

1. Line a baking sheet with a silicon mat. Fit a piping bag with a cuppler and then a piping tip.

2. Grab a mixing bowl with measured and dried egg whites done earlier in the day. Whisk in the mixer until stiff peaks form, adding food color powder during this process.

3. In your food processor bowl, combine your dried and cooled almond flour along with your powdered sugar. Pulse a few times to combine, stir and pulse a few more times to fully combine.

4. Remove your bowl of stiff meringue, place sifter over bowl and add half dry ingredient mixture and sifting on top of meringue. Fold in lightly with a spatula, scraping around the bowl then through the center. Sift remaining dry ingredients and incorporate this same way, using the spatula to scrape around the bowl and then through the center. When this stirring or macaronage is complete, batter will fall in a smooth ribbon when lifted with the spatula.

5. Place piping bag with tip into a large mug or cup to hold as you pour half of batter pipe rounds into the center of the baking mat circle outlines. Hold piping bag perpendicular to the mat, squeeze steadily. To stop flow, stop squeezing and swipe quickly to create a smooth top. Once entire pan is piped, tap pan using both hands 2-3 times against table, then use cake tester to pop air bubbles.

6. Preheat oven to 300, an internal oven thermometer will help as you will want to find out if your oven runs hot or cold. You may need to set your over at 305, to get the internal thermometer to 300. This will take some adjustments.

7. Set pan aside to dry. You will want to touch the top of the cookie to ensure slightly firm and dry before baking.

8. Bake at 300 degrees for 18 minutes on middle rack, each pan baked individually.

9. While macarons cool, beat butter in stand mixer using the paddle attachment. You will want the butter to be room temperature and it will be pale and fluffy when done. It is best to let it whip and go do something else. Add remaining buttercream ingredients when proper whipped butter has been achieved. Put into a piping bag.

10. Use some chocolate buttercream to seal the bottom of each cookie, then pipe a circle and fill with strawberry center. Placing a thin barrier of buttercream between the cookie and the strawberry center will prevent leaking.

Cookie and Cream Macaron

A cookies and cream shell, filled with cookies and cream butter cream. All gluten free, all the time.

Makes | 30 macarons

FOR THE SHELLS

- 165g egg whites
- 136g caster sugar
- 180g almond flour
- 174.5g powdered sugar
- 1/32 tsp red food color powder
- 4-5 gluten free Oreos, center scraped out and saved. Finely pulsed in food processor.

FOR THE FILLING

- 2 sticks salted butter, room temperature
- 2.5 cups powdered sugar
- 5-6 gluten free Oreos + scraped out center from Oreos added to shell

DIRECTIONS

1. Line a baking sheet with a silicon mat. Fit a piping bag with a cuppler and then a piping tip.

2. Grab a mixing bowl with measured and dried egg whites done earlier in the day. Whisk in the mixer until stiff peaks form, adding food color powder during this process.

3. In your food processor bowl, combine your dried and cooled almond flour along with your powdered sugar. Pulse a few times to combine, stir to fully combine and pulse a few more times to fully combine adding in the Oreo crumbs.

4. Remove your bowl of stiff meringue, place sifter over bowl and add half dry ingredient mixture and sifting on top of meringue. Fold in lightly with a spatula, scraping around the bowl then through the center. Sift remaining dry ingredients and incorporate this same way, using the spatula to scrape around the bowl and then through the center. When this stirring or macaronage is complete, batter will fall in a smooth ribbon when lifted with the spatula.

5. Place piping bag with tip into a large mug or cup to hold as you pour half of batter pipe rounds into the center of the baking mat circle outlines. Hold piping bag perpendicular to the mat, squeeze steadily. To stop flow, stop squeezing and swipe quickly to create a smooth top. Once entire pan is piped, tap pan using both hands 2-3 times against table, then use cake tester to pop air bubbles and swirl to make top smooth.

6. Preheat oven to 300, an internal oven thermometer will help as you will want to find out if your oven runs hot or cold. You may need to set your over at 305, to get the internal thermometer to 300. This will take some adjustments.

7. Set pan aside to dry. You will want to touch the top of the cookie to ensure slightly firm and dry before baking.

8. Bake at 300 degrees for 18 minutes on middle rack, each pan baked individually.

9. While macarons cool, beat butter in stand mixer using the paddle attachment. You will want the butter to be room temperature and it will be pale and fluffy when done. It is best to let it whip and go do something else. Add remaining buttercream ingredients when proper whipped butter has been achieved. Put into a piping bag and match macaron cookies and fill.

Star Crunch Macaron

Filled with a homemade star crunch filling, a childhood spin on a sophisticated cookie. Caramel, marshmallow, rice crispy goodness.

Makes | 30 macarons

FOR THE SHELLS

- 165g egg whites
- 136g caster sugar
- 180g almond flour
- 174.5g powdered sugar
- 1/32 tsp. of both sapphire sky and french blue food color powder
- ½ Tbs cocoa powder

FOR THE FILLING

- Cook on stove top like making rice crispies
- 1 stick of salted butter ½ cup cocoa powder 1 tsp vanilla
- 14 oz sweetened condensed milk
- 5 ½ cups rice krispy cereal 1 ¼ cup caramel bits

DIRECTIONS

1. Line a baking sheet with a silicon mat. Fit a piping bag with a cuppler and then a piping tip.

2. Grab a mixing bowl with measured and dried egg whites done earlier in the day. Whisk in the mixer until stiff peaks form, adding food color powder during this process.

3. In your food processer bowl, combine your dried and cooled almond flour along with your powdered sugar. Pulse a few times to combine, stir to fully combine and pulse a few more times to fully combine.

4. Remove your bowl of stiff meringue, place sifter over bowl and add half dry ingredient mixture and sifting on top of meringue. Fold in lightly with a spatula, scraping around the bowl then through the center. Sift remaining dry ingredients and incorporate this same way, using the spatula to scrape around the bowl and then through the center. When this stirring or macaronage is complete, batter will fall in a smooth ribbon when lifted with the spatula.

5. Place piping bag with tip into a large mug or cup to hold as you pour half of batter pipe rounds into the center of the baking mat circle outlines. Hold piping bag perpendicular to the mat, squeeze steadily. To stop flow, stop squeezing and swipe quickly to create a smooth top. Once entire pan is piped, tap pan using both hands 2-3 times against table, then use cake tester to pop air bubbles and swirl to make top smooth.

6. Preheat oven to 300, an internal oven thermometer will help as you will want to find out if your oven runs hot or cold. You may need to set your over at 305, to get the internal thermometer to 300. This will take some adjustments.

7. Set pan aside to dry. You will want to touch the top of the cookie to ensure slightly firm and dry before baking.

8. Bake at 300 degrees for 18 minutes on middle rack, each sheet pan must be baked separately.

9. Once macarons are cool, make filling on stove top. While still pretty warm, spoon ½ Tbs amounts onto a macaron and sandwich together.

Mint Chocolate Macaron

A cookie and cream + mint dream.

Makes | 30 macarons

FOR THE SHELLS

- 165g egg whites
- 136g caster sugar
- 180g almond flour
- 174.5g powdered sugar
- 1/32 tsp emerald food color powder
- 4-5 gluten free Oreos, center scraped out and saved. Finely pulsed in food processor.

FOR THE FILLING

- 2 sticks salted butter, room temperature
- 2.5 cups powdered sugar ½ tsp mint extract
- 5-6 gluten free Oreos + scraped out center from Oreos added to shell

DIRECTIONS

1. Line a baking sheet with a silicon mat. Fit a piping bag with a cuppler and then a piping tip.

2. Grab a mixing bowl with measured and dried egg whites done earlier in the day. Whisk in the mixer until stiff peaks form, adding food color powder during this process.

3. In your food processor bowl, combine your dried and cooled almond flour along with your powdered sugar. Pulse a few times to combine, stir and pulse a few more times to fully combine adding in the Oreo crumbs.

4. Remove your bowl of stiff meringue, place sifter over bowl and add half dry ingredient mixture and sifting on top of meringue. Fold in lightly with a spatula, scraping around the bowl then through the center. Sift remaining dry ingredients and incorporate this same way, using the spatula to scrape around the bowl and then through the center. When this stirring or macaronage is complete, batter will fall in a smooth ribbon when lifted with the spatula.

5. Place piping bag with tip into a large mug or cup to hold as you pour half of batter pipe rounds into the center of the baking mat circle outlines. Hold piping bag perpendicular to the mat, squeeze steadily. To stop flow, stop squeezing and swipe quickly to create a smooth top. Once entire pan is piped, tap pan using both hands 2-3 times against table, then use cake tester to pop air bubbles and swirl to make top smooth.

6. Preheat oven to 300, an internal oven thermometer will help as you will want to find out if your oven runs hot or cold. You may need to set your over at 305, to get the internal thermometer to 300. This will take some adjustments.

7. Set pan aside to dry. You will want to touch the top of the cookie to ensure slightly firm and dry before baking.

8. Bake at 300 degrees for 18 minutes on middle rack, each pan baked separately.

9. While macarons cool, beat butter in stand mixer using the paddle attachment. You will want the butter to be room temperature and it will be pale and fluffy when done. It is best to let it whip and go do something else. Add remaining buttercream ingredients when proper whipped butter has been achieved. Put into a piping bag and match macaron cookies and fill.

Chocolate Hazelnut Macaron

Chocolate macaron shell filled with Nutella Buttercream, and crunchy spinkles. Its a multi-sensory expreience.

Makes | 30 macarons

FOR THE SHELLS

- 165g egg whites
- 136g caster sugar
- 180g almond flour
- 174.5g powdered sugar
- ½ Tbs cocoa powder
- ¼ + 1/8 Tsp true brown food color powder
- Chocolate Jimmies sprinkles or chopped hazelnuts

FOR THE FILLING

- 2 sticks salted butter, room temperature
- 2 cups powdered sugar
- 1 container chocolate hazelnut spread
- 1 Tbs heavy cream

DIRECTIONS

1. Line a baking sheet with a silicon mat. Fit a piping bag with a cuppler and then a piping tip.

2. Grab a mixing bowl with measured and dried egg whites done earlier in the day. Whisk in the mixer until stiff peaks form, adding food color powder during this process.

3. In your food processor bowl, combine your dried and cooled almond flour along with your powdered sugar. Pulse a few times to combine, stir and pulse a few more times to fully combine.

4. Remove your bowl of stiff meringue, place sifter over bowl and add half dry ingredient mixture and sifting on top of meringue. Fold in lightly with a spatula, scraping around the bowl then through the center. Sift remaining dry ingredients and incorporate this same way, using the spatula to scrape around the bowl and then through the center. When this stirring or macaronage is complete, batter will fall in a smooth ribbon when lifted with the spatula.

5. Place piping bag with tip into a large mug or cup to hold as you pour half of batter pipe rounds into the center of the baking mat circle outlines. Hold piping bag perpendicular to the mat, squeeze steadily. To stop flow, stop squeezing and swipe quickly to create a smooth top. Once entire pan is piped, tap pan using both hands 2-3 times against table, then use cake tester to pop air bubbles and swirl to make top smooth. Sprinkle with nonpareils.

6. Preheat oven to 300, an internal oven thermometer will help as you will want to find out if your oven runs hot or cold. You may need to set your over at 305, to get the internal thermometer to 300. This will take some adjustments.

7. Set pan aside to dry. You will want to touch the top of the cookie to ensure slightly firm and dry before baking.

8. Bake at 300 degrees for 18 minutes on middle rack, each sheet pan must be baked separately.

9. While macarons cool, beat butter in stand mixer using the paddle attachment. You will want the butter to be room temperature and it will be pale and fluffy when done. It is best to let it whip and go do something else. Add remaining buttercream ingredients when proper whipped butter has been achieved. Put into a piping bag and match macaron cookies and fill.

Vanilla Bean Caramel Macaron

Homemade vanilla caramel center, and a circled by light vanilla bean buttercream. A definite favorite among many, delicious is delivered.

Makes | 30 macarons

FOR THE SHELLS

- 165g egg whites
- 136g caster sugar
- 180g almond flour
- 174.5g powdered sugar
- 1/64 tsp lilac food color powder
- Hot pink nonpareil sprinkles

FOR THE BUTTERCREAM FILLING

- 2 sticks salted butter, room temperature
- 3 cups powdered sugar
- 3 tsp vanilla bean paste

FOR THE CARAMEL CENTER

- ¼ cup water
- 250g caster sugar
- 60g light corn syrup
- 3/4 cup heavy cream
- 3 Tbs salted butter
- ½ tsp salt

DIRECTIONS

1. Line a baking sheet with a silicon mat. Fit a piping bag with a cuppler and then a piping tip.

2. Grab a mixing bowl with measured and dried egg whites done earlier in the day. Whisk in the mixer until stiff peaks form, adding food color powder during this process.

3. In your food processer bowl, combine your dried and cooled almond flour along with your powdered sugar. Pulse a few times to combine, stir and pulse a few more times to fully combine.

4. Remove your bowl of stiff meringue, place sifter over bowl and add half dry ingredient mixture and sifting on top of meringue. Fold in lightly with a spatula, scraping around the bowl then through the center. Sift remaining dry ingredients and incorporate this same way, using the spatula to scrape around the bowl and then through the center. When this stirring or macaronage is complete, batter will fall in a smooth ribbon when lifted with the spatula.

5. Place piping bag with tip into a large mug or cup to hold as you pour half of batter pipe rounds into the center of the baking mat circle outlines. Hold piping bag perpendicular to the mat, squeeze steadily. To stop flow, stop squeezing and swipe quickly to create a smooth top. Once entire pan is piped, tap pan using both hands 2-3 times against table, then use cake tester to pop air bubbles.

6. Preheat oven to 300, an internal oven thermometer will help as you will want to find out if your oven runs hot or cold. You may need to set your over at 305, to get the internal thermometer to 300. This will take some adjustments.

7. Set pan aside to dry. You will want to touch the top of the cookie to ensure slightly firm and dry before baking.

8. Bake at 300 degrees for 18 minutes on middle rack, each pan baked separately.

9. While macarons cool, make caramel for center by adding water, sugar and corn syrup in saucepan, bring to a boil until caramel brown in color, remove from heat and stir in heavy cream, butter and salt, continue to stir to combine, then set aside to cool. Beat butter in stand mixer to make vanilla bean buttercream. You will want the butter to be room temperature and it will be pale and fluffy when done. It is best to let it whip and go do something else. Add remaining buttercream ingredients when proper whipped butter has been achieved. Put into a piping bag and match macaron cookies and fill.

TEAS, SPICE

& FLORAL

Carrot Cake Macaron

Carrot Cake spiced macaron filled with cream cheese icing. My husbands favorite.

Makes | 30 macarons

FOR THE SHELLS

- 165g egg whites
- 136g caster sugar
- 180g almond flour
- 174.5g powdered sugar
- 1/32 tsp sunshine food color powder
- 1/32 red rose food color powder
- ¼ tsp cinnamon
- ¼ tsp nutmeg

FOR THE FILLING

- 1 sticks salted butter, room temperature
- 1 block cream cheese 1 tsp. vanilla extract ½ tsp cinnamon
- ½ tsp nutmeg
- 3 ½ cup powdered sugar
- ½ cup dehydrated carrot (rehydrated and pulsed in food processor)

DIRECTIONS

1. Line a baking sheet with a silicon mat. Fit a piping bag with a cuppler and then a piping tip.

2. Grab a mixing bowl with measured and dried egg whites done earlier in the day. Whisk in the mixer until stiff peaks form, adding food color powder during this process.

3. In your food processor bowl, combine your dried and cooled almond flour along with your powdered sugar. Pulse a few times to combine, stir and pulse a few more times to fully combine.

4. Remove your bowl of stiff meringue, place sifter over bowl and add half dry ingredient mixture and sifting on top of meringue. Fold in lightly with a spatula, scraping around the bowl then through the center. Sift remaining dry ingredients and incorporate this same way, using the spatula to scrape around the bowl and then through the center. When this stirring or macaronage is complete, batter will fall in a smooth ribbon when lifted with the spatula.

5. Place piping bag with tip into a large mug or cup to hold as you pour half of batter pipe rounds into the center of the baking mat circle outlines. Hold piping bag perpendicular to the mat, squeeze steadily. To stop flow, stop squeezing and swipe quickly to create a smooth top. Once entire pan is piped, tap pan using both hands 2-3 times against table, then use cake tester to pop air bubbles and swirl to make top smooth.

6. Preheat oven to 300, an internal oven thermometer will help as you will want to find out if your oven runs hot or cold. You may need to set your over at 305, to get the internal thermometer to 300. This will take some adjustments.

7. Set pan aside to dry. You will want to touch the top of the cookie to ensure slightly firm and dry before baking.

8. Bake at 300 degrees for 18 minutes on middle rack, each pan baked separately.

9. While macarons cool, beat butter in stand mixer using the paddle attachment. You will want the butter to be room temperature and it will be pale and fluffy when done. It is best to let it whip and go do something else. Add remaining buttercream ingredients when proper whipped butter has been achieved. Put into a piping bag and match macaron cookies and fill.

Coconut Cream Macaron

Toasted coconut buttercream made with coconut milk and freshly toasted coconut.

Makes | 30 macarons

FOR THE SHELLS

- 165g egg whites
- 136g caster sugar
- 180g almond flour
- 174.5g powdered sugar
- 1/64 tsp red rose food color powder
- Sprinkled with sweetened shredded coconut, it will become lightly toasted in the oven

FOR THE FILLING

- 2 sticks salted butter, room temperature
- 2 cups powdered sugar
- 4 Tbs sweetened condensed coconut milk
- ¾ cup toasted coconut

DIRECTIONS

1. Line a baking sheet with a silicon mat. Fit a piping bag with a cuppler and then a piping tip.

2. Grab a mixing bowl with measured and dried egg whites done earlier in the day. Whisk in the mixer until stiff peaks form, adding food color powder during this process.

3. In your food processor bowl, combine your dried and cooled almond flour along with your powdered sugar. Pulse a few times to combine, stir and pulse a few more times to fully combine.

4. Remove your bowl of stiff meringue, place sifter over bowl and add half dry ingredient mixture and sifting on top of meringue. Fold in lightly with a spatula, scraping around the bowl then through the center. Sift remaining dry ingredients and incorporate this same way, using the spatula to scrape around the bowl and then through the center. When this stirring or macaronage is complete, batter will fall in a smooth ribbon when lifted with the spatula.

5. Place piping bag with tip into a large mug or cup to hold as you pour half of batter pipe rounds into the center of the baking mat circle outlines. Hold piping bag perpendicular to the mat, squeeze steadily.

To stop flow, stop squeezing and swipe quickly to create a smooth top. Once entire pan is piped, tap pan using both hands 2-3 times against table, then use cake tester to pop air bubbles and swirl to make top smooth. Sprinkle with toasted coconut.

6. Preheat oven to 300, an internal oven thermometer will help as you will want to find out if your oven runs hot or cold. You may need to set your over at 305, to get the internal thermometer to 300. This will take some adjustments.

7. Set pan aside to dry. You will want to touch the top of the cookie to ensure slightly firm and dry before baking.

8. Bake at 300 degrees for 18 minutes on middle rack, each pan baked separately.

9. While macarons cool, beat butter in stand mixer using the paddle attachment. You will want the butter to be room temperature and it will be pale and fluffy when done. It is best to let it whip and go do something else. Add remaining buttercream ingredients when proper whipped butter has been achieved. Put into a piping bag and match macaron cookies and fill.

Matcha Macaron

Matcha flavored shell sandwiching a sweet matcha buttercream.

Makes | 30 macarons

FOR THE SHELLS

- 165g egg whites
- 136g caster sugar
- 180g almond flour
- 174.5g powdered sugar
- 1/32 tsp soldier green food color powder
- ¼ tsp matcha powder

FOR THE FILLING

- 2 sticks salted butter, room temperature
- 2.5 cups powdered sugar
- 2 tsp matcha powder
- 2 tsp vanilla extract

DIRECTIONS

1. Line a baking sheet with a silicon mat. Fit a piping bag with a cuppler and then a piping tip.

2. Grab a mixing bowl with measured and dried egg whites done earlier in the day. Whisk in the mixer until stiff peaks form, adding food color powder during this process.

3. In your food processor bowl, combine your dried and cooled almond flour along with your powdered sugar. Pulse a few times to combine, stir and pulse a few more times to fully combine.

4. Remove your bowl of stiff meringue, place sifter over bowl and add half dry ingredient mixture and sifting on top of meringue. Fold in lightly with a spatula, scraping around the bowl then through the center. Sift remaining dry ingredients and incorporate this same way, using the spatula to scrape around the bowl and then through the center. When this stirring or macaronage is complete, batter will fall in a smooth ribbon when lifted with the spatula.

1. Place piping bag with tip into a large mug or cup to hold as you pour half of batter pipe rounds into the center of the baking mat circle outlines. Hold piping bag perpendicular to the mat, squeeze steadily. To stop flow, stop squeezing and swipe quickly to create a smooth top. Once entire pan is piped, tap pan using both hands 2-3 times against table, then use cake tester to pop air bubbles and swirl to make top smooth.

2. Preheat oven to 300, an internal oven thermometer will help as you will want to find out if your oven runs hot or cold. You may need to set your over at 305, to get the internal thermometer to 300. This will take some adjustments.

3. Set pan aside to dry. You will want to touch the top of the cookie to ensure slightly firm and dry before baking.

1. Bake at 300 degrees for 18 minutes on middle rack, each pan baked separately.

2. While macarons cool, beat butter in stand mixer using the paddle attachment. You will want the butter to be room temperature and it will be pale and fluffy when done. It is best to let it whip and go do something else. Add remaining buttercream ingredients when proper whipped butter has been achieved. Put into a piping bag and match macaron cookies and fill.

Pistachio White Choc. Macaron

A perfectly balanced salty sweet macaron, using pistachio nuts and a white chocolate center.

Makes | 30 macarons

FOR THE SHELLS

- 165g egg whites
- 136g caster sugar
- 180g almond flour
- 174.5g powdered sugar ¼ Tsp white food color gel
- Sprinkle with crushed pistachio nuts

FOR THE FILLING

- 2 sticks salted butter, room temperature
- 3 cups powdered sugar ¾ tsp salt
- ¾ cup crushed pistachio nuts
- Fill with premium white Ghirardelli white chocolate sauce

DIRECTIONS

1. Line a baking sheet with a silicon mat. Fit a piping bag with a cuppler and then a piping tip.

2. Grab a mixing bowl with measured and dried egg whites done earlier in the day. Whisk in the mixer until stiff peaks form, adding food color powder during this process.

3. In your food processor bowl, combine your dried and cooled almond flour along with your powdered sugar. Pulse a few times to combine, stir and pulse a few more times to fully combine.

4. Remove your bowl of stiff meringue, place sifter over bowl and add half dry ingredient mixture and sifting on top of meringue. Fold in lightly with a spatula, scraping around the bowl then through the center. Sift remaining dry ingredients and incorporate this same way, using the spatula to scrape around the bowl and then through the center. When this stirring or macaronage is complete, batter will fall in a smooth ribbon when lifted with the spatula.

5. Place piping bag with tip into a large mug or cup to hold as you pour half of batter pipe rounds into the center of the baking mat circle outlines. Hold piping bag perpendicular to the mat, squeeze steadily. To stop flow, stop squeezing and swipe quickly to create a smooth top. Once entire pan is piped, tap pan using both hands 2-3 times against table, then use cake tester to pop air bubbles. Sprinkle with nuts.

6. Preheat oven to 300, an internal oven thermometer will help as you will want to find out if your oven runs hot or cold. You may need to set your over at 305, to get the internal thermometer to 300. This will take some adjustments.

7. Set pan aside to dry. You will want to touch the top of the cookie to ensure slightly firm and dry before baking.

8. Bake at 300 degrees for 18 minutes on middle rack, each pan baked separately.

9. While macarons cool, make pistachio buttercream. You will want to create a barrier by swiping a thin layer of buttercream on each shell before piping a circle of buttercream and filing with the white chocolate enter. This will help cookie from leaking during maturation. Put into a piping bag and match macaron cookies and fill.

Pumpkin Pie Macaron

Exactly that, a pumpkin spiced shell and buttercream with a whip cream center.

Makes | 30 macarons

FOR THE SHELLS

- 165g egg whites
- 136g caster sugar
- 180g almond flour
- 174.5g powdered sugar
- 12 drops orange food gel color
- 1/32 redwood food color powder

FOR THE FILLING

- 2 sticks salted butter, room temperature
- 3 cups powdered sugar
- 2 tsp pumpkin pie spice
- ½ cup cold pumpkin pie mix
- ¼ tsp ginger spice
- ¼ tsp cinnamon

FOR THE WHIP CREAM FILLING

- Store bought whip cream for the center or go for it – make your own

DIRECTIONS

1. Line a baking sheet with a silicon mat. Fit a piping bag with a cuppler and then a piping tip.

2. Grab a mixing bowl with measured and dried egg whites done earlier in the day. Whisk in the mixer until stiff peaks form, adding food color powder during this process.

3. In your food processor bowl, combine your dried and cooled almond flour along with your powdered sugar. Pulse a few times to combine, stir and pulse a few more times to fully combine.

4. Remove your bowl of stiff meringue, place sifter over bowl and add half dry ingredient mixture and sifting on top of meringue. Fold in lightly with a spatula, scraping around the bowl then through the center. Sift remaining dry ingredients and incorporate this same way, using the spatula to scrape around the bowl and then through the center. When this stirring or macaronage is complete, batter will fall in a smooth ribbon when lifted with the spatula.

5. Place piping bag with tip into a large mug or cup to hold as you pour half of batter pipe rounds into the center of the baking mat circle outlines. Hold piping bag perpendicular to the mat, squeeze steadily. To stop flow, stop squeezing and swipe quickly to create a smooth top. Once entire pan is piped, tap pan using both hands 2-3 times against table, then use cake tester to pop air bubbles.

6. Preheat oven to 300, an internal oven thermometer will help as you will want to find out if your oven runs hot or cold. You may need to set your over at 305, to get the internal thermometer to 300. This will take some adjustments.

7. Set pan aside to dry. You will want to touch the top of the cookie to ensure slightly firm and dry before baking.

8. Bake at 300 degrees for 18 minutes on middle rack, each pan baked separately.

9. While macarons cool, beat butter in stand mixer using the paddle attachment. You will want the butter to be room temperature and it will be pale and fluffy when done. It is best to let it whip and go do something else. Add remaining buttercream ingredients when proper whipped butter has been achieved. No buttercream barrier needed for this recipe. Circle that buttercream and fill with whip cream.

Dirty Chai Macaron

A Chai Tea and espresso spiced shell filled with a creamy chai buttercream.

Makes | 30 macarons

FOR THE SHELLS

- 165g egg whites
- 136g caster sugar
- 180g almond flour
- 174.5g powdered sugar
- 1/8 blueberry food color powder
- 1 chai tea bag, processed along flour and powdered sugar
- Sprinkle with espresso powder

FOR THE FILLING

- 2 sticks salted butter, room temperature
- 3 cups powdered sugar
- 1 tsp vanilla extract
- 1 chai tea bag, powdered in spice grinder

DIRECTIONS

1. Line a baking sheet with a silicon mat. Fit a piping bag with a cuppler and then a piping tip.

2. Grab a mixing bowl with measured and dried egg whites done earlier in the day. Whisk in the mixer until stiff peaks form, adding food color powder during this process.

3. In your food processor bowl, combine your dried and cooled almond flour along with your powdered sugar. Pulse a few times to combine, stir pulse again to fully combine adding in contents of 1 chai tea bag.

4. Remove your bowl of stiff meringue, place sifter over bowl and add half dry ingredient mixture and sifting on top of meringue. Fold in lightly with a spatula, scraping around the bowl then through the center. Sift remaining dry ingredients and incorporate this same way, using the spatula to scrape around the bowl and then through the center. When this stirring or macaronage is complete, batter will fall in a smooth ribbon when lifted with the spatula.

5. Place piping bag with tip into a large mug or cup to hold as you pour half of batter pipe rounds into the center of the baking mat circle outlines. Hold piping bag perpendicular to the mat, squeeze steadily. To stop flow, stop squeezing and swipe quickly to create a smooth top. Once entire pan is piped, tap pan using both hands 2-3 times against table, then use cake tester to pop air bubbles and swirl to make top smooth. Sprinkle with espresso powder.

6. Preheat oven to 300, an internal oven thermometer will help as you will want to find out if your oven runs hot or cold. You may need to set your over at 305, to get the internal thermometer to 300. This will take some adjustments.

7. Set pan aside to dry. You will want to touch the top of the cookie to ensure slightly firm and dry before baking.

8. Bake at 300 degrees for 18 minutes on middle rack, each pan baked separately.

9. While macarons cool, beat butter in stand mixer using the paddle attachment. You will want the butter to be room temperature and it will be pale and fluffy when done. It is best to let it whip and go do something else. Add remaining buttercream ingredients when proper whipped butter has been achieved. Put into a piping bag and match macaron cookies and fill.

Cinnamon Toast Macaron

Really a favorite, giving both fall and cinnamon cereal loving vibes.

Makes | 30 macarons

FOR THE SHELLS

- 165g egg whites
- 136g caster sugar
- 180g almond flour
- 174.5g powdered sugar
- 2¼ white food color powder
- Sprinkle with cinnamon sugar mix
- *Paint 3 stripes up the piping bag using brown gel food color to produce the swirl.

FOR THE FILLING

- 2 sticks salted butter, room temperature
- 3 cups powdered sugar
- 2 tsp cinnamon
- 2 tsp vanilla extract

DIRECTIONS

1. Line a baking sheet with a silicon mat. Fit a piping bag with a cuppler and then a piping tip.

2. Grab a mixing bowl with measured and dried egg whites done earlier in the day. Whisk in the mixer until stiff peaks form, adding food color powder during this process.

3. In your food processor bowl, combine your dried and cooled almond flour along with your powdered sugar. Pulse a few times to combine, stir and pulse a few more times to fully combine.

4. Remove your bowl of stiff meringue, place sifter over bowl and add half dry ingredient mixture and sifting on top of meringue. Fold in lightly with a spatula, scraping around the bowl then through the center. Sift remaining dry ingredients and incorporate this same way, using the spatula to scrape around the bowl and then through the center. When this stirring or macaronage is complete, batter will fall in a smooth ribbon when lifted with the spatula.

5. Place piping bag with tip into a large mug or cup to hold as you pour half of batter pipe rounds into the center of the baking mat circle outlines.

6. Remember the bag has been striped with 3 brown gel lines, pipe rounds into the center of the making mat circle outlines.

Hold piping bag perpendicular to the mat, squeeze steadily. The 3 stripes will produce an brown swirl.

7. To stop flow, stop squeezing and swipe quickly to create a smooth top. Once entire pan is piped, tap pan using both hands 2-3 times against table, then use cake tester to pop air bubbles and swirl to make top smooth. Sprinkle with cinnamon sugar.

8. Preheat oven to 300, an internal oven thermometer will help as you will want to find out if your oven runs hot or cold. You may need to set your over at 305, to get the internal thermometer to 300. This will take some adjustments.

9. Set pan aside to dry. You will want to touch the top of the cookie to ensure slightly firm and dry before baking.

10. Bake at 300 degrees for 18 minutes on middle rack, each pan baked separately.

11. While macarons cool, beat butter in stand mixer using the paddle attachment. You will want the butter to be room temperature and it will be pale and fluffy when done. It is best to let it whip and go do something else. Add remaining buttercream ingredients when proper whipped butter has been achieved. Put into a piping bag and match macaron cookies and fill.

PSL Macaron

Espresso and pumpkin spice flavored shell filled with pumpkin spice marshmallow buttercream. Pumpkin Spice Latte lovers unite!

Makes | 30 macarons

FOR THE SHELLS

- 165g egg whites
- 136g caster sugar
- 180g almond flour
- 174.5g powdered sugar
- 1/8 tsp autumn gold food color powder
- 6 drops orange gel food color
- 1/64 redwood food color powder
- ½ tsp pumpkin spice
- Espresso powder for sprinkling

FOR THE FILLING

- 2 sticks salted butter, room temperature
- 2 cups powdered sugar
- 13 oz marshmallow fluff
- 3 tsp espresso powder
- 1 tsp pumpkin spice

DIRECTIONS

1. Line a baking sheet with a silicon mat. Fit a piping bag with a cuppler and then a piping tip.

2. Grab a mixing bowl with measured and dried egg whites done earlier in the day. Whisk in the mixer until stiff peaks form, adding food color powder during this process.

3. In your food processor bowl, combine your dried and cooled almond flour along with your powdered sugar. Pulse a few times to combine, stir and pulse a few more times to fully combine.

4. Remove your bowl of stiff meringue, place sifter over bowl and add half dry ingredient mixture and sifting on top of meringue. Fold in lightly with a spatula, scraping around the bowl then through the center. Sift remaining dry ingredients and incorporate this same way, using the spatula to scrape around the bowl and then through the center. When this stirring or macaronage is complete, batter will fall in a smooth ribbon when lifted with the spatula.

5. Place piping bag with tip into a large mug or cup to hold as you pour half of batter pipe rounds into the center of the baking mat circle outlines. Hold piping bag perpendicular to the mat, squeeze steadily. To stop flow, stop squeezing and swipe quickly to create a smooth top. Once entire pan is piped, tap pan using both hands 2-3 times against table, then use cake tester to pop air bubbles. Sprinkle with espresso powder.

6. Preheat oven to 300, an internal oven thermometer will help as you will want to find out if your oven runs hot or cold. You may need to set your over at 305, to get the internal thermometer to 300. This will take some adjustments.

7. Set pan aside to dry. You will want to touch the top of the cookie to ensure slightly firm and dry before baking.

8. Bake at 300 degrees for 18 minutes on middle rack, each pan baked separately.

9. While macarons cool, beat butter in stand mixer using the paddle attachment. You will want the butter to be room temperature and it will be pale and fluffy when done.

10. It is best to let it whip and go do something else. Add in powdered sugar first, and once fully creamed add remaining buttercream ingredients. Put into a piping bag and match macaron cookies and fill.

Lavender Macaron

Real dried lavender processed right into the shell and filled with a light vanilla buttercream.

Makes | 30 macarons

FOR THE SHELLS

- 165g egg whites
- 136g caster sugar
- 180g almond flour
- 174.5g powdered sugar
- 1 Tbs food grade lavender flowers, added to almond flour
- *Top with a lavender flower or two for decoration

FOR THE FILLING

- 2 sticks salted butter, room temperature
- 3 cups powdered sugar 1 tsp vanilla extract

DIRECTIONS

1. Line a baking sheet with a silicon mat. Fit a piping bag with a cuppler and then a piping tip.

2. Grab a mixing bowl with measured and dried egg whites done earlier in the day. Whisk in the mixer until stiff peaks form, adding food color powder during this process.

3. In your food processor bowl, combine your dried and cooled almond flour along with your powdered sugar. Pulse a few times to combine, stir and pulse a few more times to fully combine.

4. Remove your bowl of stiff meringue, place sifter over bowl and add half dry ingredient mixture and sifting on top of meringue. Fold in lightly with a spatula, scraping around the bowl then through the center. Sift remaining dry ingredients and incorporate this same way, using the spatula to scrape around the bowl and then through the center. When this stirring or macaronage is complete, batter will fall in a smooth ribbon when lifted with the spatula.

5. Place piping bag with tip into a large mug or cup to hold as you pour half of batter pipe rounds into the center of the baking mat circle outlines. Hold piping bag perpendicular to the mat, squeeze steadily. To stop flow, stop squeezing and swipe quickly to create a smooth top. Once entire pan is piped, tap pan using both hands 2-3 times against table, then use cake tester to pop air bubbles and swirl to make top smooth. Top with 1-2 lavender flowers.

6. Preheat oven to 300, an internal oven thermometer will help as you will want to find out if your oven runs hot or cold. You may need to set your over at 305, to get the internal thermometer to 300. This will take some adjustments.

7. Set pan aside to dry. You will want to touch the top of the cookie to ensure slightly firm and dry before baking.

8. Bake at 300 degrees for 18 minutes on middle rack, each pan baked separately.

9. While macarons cool, beat butter in stand mixer using the paddle attachment. You will want the butter to be room temperature and it will be pale and fluffy when done. It is best to let it whip and go do something else. Add remaining buttercream ingredients when proper whipped butter has been achieved. Put into a piping bag and match macaron cookies and fill.

Peppermint Macaron

Peppermint flavored shell delightfully swirled and filled with peppermint buttercream. Finish them off with a dash of edible glitter for that holiday sparkle.

Makes | 30 macarons

FOR THE SHELLS

- 165g egg whites
- 136g caster sugar
- 180g almond flour
- 174.5g powdered sugar
- 1/16 tsp peppermint extract
- *Too much more than this will ruin the meringue consistency
- 2 ¼ tsp White food color powder
- *3 stripes of red gel in piping bag for swirl pattern

FOR THE FILLING

- 2 sticks salted butter, room temperature
- 3 cups powdered sugar
- 1 tsp peppermint extract
- *BE EXTRA! Add edible glitter to make is sparkle after filling.

DIRECTIONS

1. Line a baking sheet with a silicon mat. Fit a piping bag with a cuppler and then a piping tip.

2. Grab a mixing bowl with measured and dried egg whites done earlier in the day. Whisk in the mixer until stiff peaks form, adding food color powder during this process.

3. In your food processor bowl, combine your dried and cooled almond flour along with your powdered sugar. Pulse a few times to combine, stir and pulse a few more times to fully combine.

4. Remove your bowl of stiff meringue, place sifter over bowl and add half dry ingredient mixture and sifting on top of meringue. Fold in lightly with a spatula, scraping around the bowl then through the center. Sift remaining dry ingredients and incorporate this same way, using the spatula to scrape around the bowl and then through the center. When this stirring or macaronage is complete, batter will fall in a smooth ribbon when lifted with the spatula.

5. Place piping bag with tip into a large mug or cup to hold as you pour half of batter pipe rounds into the center of the baking mat circle outlines.

6. Remember the bag has been striped with 3 red gel lines, pipe rounds into the center of the making mat circle outlines. Hold piping bag perpendicular to the mat, squeeze steadily. To stop flow, stop squeezing and swipe quickly to create a smooth top. Once entire pan is piped, tap pan using both hands 2-3 times against table, then use cake tester to pop air bubbles .

7. Preheat oven to 300, an internal oven thermometer will help as you will want to find out if your oven runs hot or cold.

8. You may need to set your over at 305, to get the internal thermometer to 300. This will take some adjustments.

9. Set pan aside to dry. You will want to touch the top of the cookie to ensure slightly firm and dry before baking.

10. Bake at 300 degrees for 18 minutes on middle rack, each pan baked separately.

11. While macarons cool, beat butter in stand mixer using the paddle attachment. You will want the butter to be room temperature and it will be pale and fluffy when done. It is best to let it whip and go do something else. Add remaining buttercream ingredients when proper whipped butter has been achieved. Put into a piping bag and match macaron cookies and fill.

Gingerbread Macaron

Gingerbread spiced shell and a slightly spicy gingerbread buttercream, topped with Christmas sprinkles – Tis the Season.

Makes | 30 macarons

FOR THE SHELLS

- 165g egg whites
- 136g caster sugar
- 180g almond flour
- 174.5g powdered sugar
- 1 tsp ground ginger
- ¾ tsp ground cinnamon
- ¼ tsp nutmeg Christmas sprinkles

FOR THE FILLING

- 2 sticks salted butter, room temperature
- 2.5 cups powdered sugar
- 2 Tbs molasses
- 1 tsp ground ginger
- 1 tsp nutmeg
- 1 tsp ground cinnamon
- 1 tsp vanilla extract

IRECTIONS

1. Line a baking sheet with a silicon mat. Fit a piping bag with a cuppler and then a piping tip.

2. Grab a mixing bowl with measured and dried egg whites done earlier in the day. Whisk in the mixer until stiff peaks form, adding food color powder during this process.

3. In your food processor bowl, combine your dried and cooled almond flour along with your powdered sugar. Pulse a few times to combine, stir and pulse a few more times to fully combine.

4. Remove your bowl of stiff meringue, place sifter over bowl and add half dry ingredient mixture and sifting on top of meringue. Fold in lightly with a spatula, scraping around the bowl then through the center. Sift remaining dry ingredients and incorporate this same way, using the spatula to scrape around the bowl and then through the center. When this stirring or macaronage is complete, batter will fall in a smooth ribbon when lifted with the spatula.

5. Place piping bag with tip into a large mug or cup to hold as you pour half of batter pipe rounds into the center of the baking mat circle outlines. Hold piping bag perpendicular to the mat, squeeze steadily. To stop flow, stop squeezing and swipe quickly to create a smooth top. Once entire pan is piped, tap pan using both hands 2-3 times against table, then use cake tester to pop air bubbles. Sprinkle with Christmas flare.

6. Preheat oven to 300, an internal oven thermometer will help as you will want to find out if your oven runs hot or cold. You may need to set your over at 305, to get the internal thermometer to 300. This will take some adjustments.

7. Set pan aside to dry. You will want to touch the top of the cookie to ensure slightly firm and dry before baking.

8. Bake at 300 degrees for 18 minutes on middle rack, each pan separately.

9. While macarons cool, beat butter in stand mixer using the paddle attachment. You will want the butter to be room temperature and it will be pale and fluffy when done. It is best to let it whip and go do something else. Add remaining buttercream ingredients when proper whipped butter has been achieved. Put into a piping bag and match macaron cookies and fill.

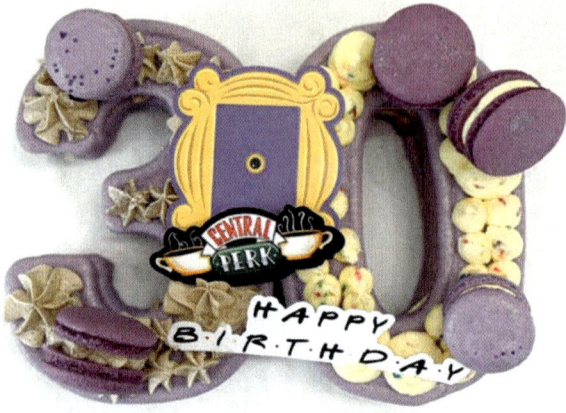

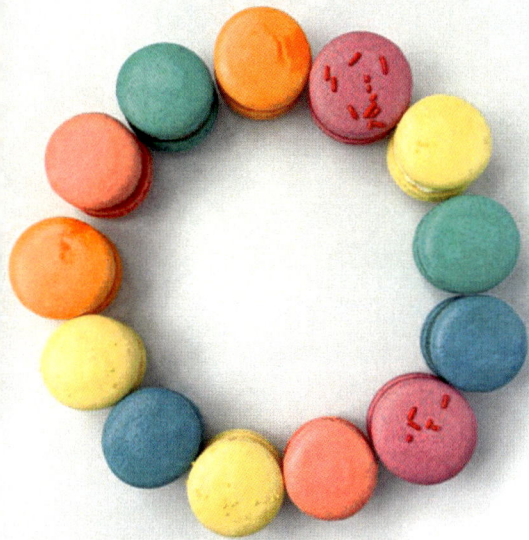

Acknowledgments

This Macaron business has been prompted and inspired by the fiercest group of women I know. They have the deepest knowing of all the struggle and thriving that has accumulated in my bones as a mother. Laurie Belleville, Kim Kruse, Kelsey Ahern. You are my people, and for it I am blessed. I would be remised if I didn't mention my husband. He washes dishes, listens to my flavor and method rambling, gives flavor suggestions, design ideas, and delivers. When I need a pep talk, he's the hype man. Ryan Fahle, you are forever, my guy. To Melissa Mckenzie from Triple M Studio and Deborah Beachy, photography extraordinaire; your creativness inspires me. And if my friend Bethany Ricks didn't take me for long rides to obscure places, I'd probably still be a human puddle. Laughter is healing.

Also, I am everyday grateful for two rescue bakers who helped when life kicked the feet out from under me. Roxanne Yoder and Bonnie McCormick. The ways in which they assisted in this book by just being available and willing to learn and organize me. Sincerely. Thank you to all deep connections I have made through macarons, my dear customers, everyone who has cheered me on. My family, my egar taste testers, my friends.
I am grateful.

An important note; the driving force for Sifted Macaron Co. is giving. 25% of macaron profits go to the non-profit Dream Makers Project. Dream Makers connects the community to the needs of youth aging out of the foster care system. They are on a mission to remove barriers that stand in the way of the empowered and connected lives these youth dream of having. Thus- the perfect fit for my heart and business.

Please go to Dreammakersproject.org to learn more about this amazing organization and how you can help.

About the Author

Randi Fahle is a wife of 18 years and mother of 2, living in mid-west Ohio. Randi obtained her bachelors in Sociology at The Ohio State Unviersity but more importantly she has a black belt in trauma parenting and an honorary degree in being herself. When she isn't working or cheering on her kids, Davontae and Obi, you guessed it, she is baking. Randi is the creative mind behind the IG account @SiftedMacaronCo, taking her own macaron photos. She began Sifted Macaron Co. having never eaten a macaron before in her life, and thats just how she rolls.

Made in the USA
Las Vegas, NV
21 June 2024